Tuktuleree

Best Wishes
Ellis M. Kand

The author dressed in traditional Inuit caribou clothing.

Tuktuleree

The Man Who Looks After The Caribou

ELLIS M. LAND

Pentland Books
Edinburgh – Cambridge – Durham – USA

First published in 2001 by
Pentland Books
1 Hutton Close
South Church
Bishop Auckland
Durham

ISBN 1-85821-938-8

Typeset in Bell 11 on 13 by
Carnegie Publishing
Carnegie House
Chatsworth Road
Lancaster
www.carnegiepub.co.uk

Printed and bound in the UK by
Bookcraft, Midsomer Norton

*To my wife Iris and
children Kevin and Tavia,
who shared the adventure
making the most isolated outpost home*

Contents

Illustrations

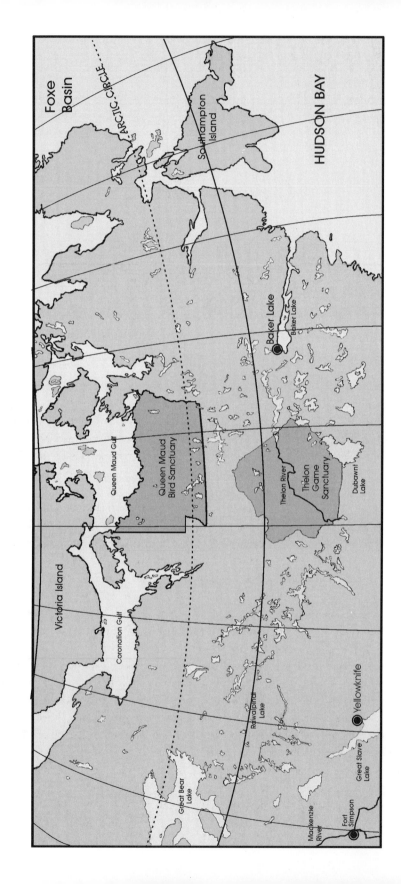

Foxe Basin

ARCTIC CIRCLE

HUDSON BAY

Southampton Island

Baker Lake

Baker Lake

Queen Maud Gulf

Queen Maud Bird Sanctuary

Thelon River

Thelon Game Sanctuary

Dubawnt Lake

Victoria Island

Coronation Gulf

Kdwalpmal Lake

Yellowknife

Great Bear Lake

Mackenzie River

Fort Simpson

Great Slave Lake

CHAPTER ONE

The Arctic Beckons

There's a land that lies waiting for you and for me
Where the distant horizon sweeps down to the sea
Like the face of a maiden that's trusting and strong
I'm in love with the Arctic; that's where I belong!

Home To The Northland

T HE SPRING of 1968 came early to the Wadena District of southern Saskatchewan. There was more than enough work to keep a Conservation Officer with the Department of Natural Resources occupied. I had been transferred to this area ten months earlier and never liked it. The gentle breath of May had turned the landscape varied shades of green and waterfowl passed daily overhead, yet I remained restless and discontented.

It had been my life-long dream to be a Conservation Officer in my home province. Achieving it had been a long and difficult struggle. Finally after graduation in 1966 I held a crisp technical diploma in Renewable Resources and a permanent position in the Pelican Narrows District of northern Saskatchewan. I couldn't believe my good fortune. Now less than two years later, I was intent on finding an acceptable way to escape.

The reason was simple enough; I was in love with a girl and the north country. Both had insidiously permeated my soul until on the verge of madness I knew I must have one or the other. I dared to dream of having both.

I had no way of knowing as I impatiently watched spring awaken the land, that in a few months I would be married and leaving with my new bride for a honeymoon on the tundra with a group of Inuit caribou hunters. It seemed quite improbable. My romance with the girl I loved hung on fine silken threads which threatened to break at the slightest vibration. We had been apart for four months. Whitehorse seemed so very far away. I was convinced when she left to work there, that I would never see her again. We had written once or twice a week at first. Her letters were full of the excitement of a new place, new friends and interesting work. Gradually our letters became less frequent. She was enjoying her new surroundings, meeting young men and dating some of them. It was as if she were in another country. I had asked her once to come back to Saskatchewan but she refused. I felt defeated, helpless, and our future together now seemed in doubt. After months of letter writing, we were becoming more distant in our discourses, and the flame that once flickered brightly was slowly dying.

I was attending an Officers' Conference in Regina when my chance to escape came so quickly and quietly that I almost missed it. A few of the officers were complaining during the break about some work related matter. I heard one officer remark, 'Well, you know you can always go to Baker Lake in the Northwest Territories if things get too bad. I see they're advertising for a Game Officer.' He sipped his coffee before continuing, 'I saw the ad in the morning paper.' Suddenly my heart began to race: this was the chance I had been waiting for.

I submitted my application for the Game Officer position as soon as I returned to Wadena. The following week I was asked to assist in the control of a large forest fire near White Swan Lake.

This development made me rather anxious as I felt I would be away when news of the Baker Lake job arrived. Fortunately a friend who shared the same office building checked my mail and contacted me by radiotelephone. An all-night drive to attend an interview in Saskatoon was necessary but happily when I returned from fire duty the Baker Lake job offer was on my desk. On 17 June I left Saskatchewan for the Northwest Territories.

The turbo-prop droned northward as I gazed with some satisfaction at the boreal forest passing steadily beneath the aircraft. I was en route to Fort Smith via Fort Chipewyan where I was to spend a week on orientation before going to Baker Lake. The air was clear and smooth and the time passed pleasantly. Off to the east I could see the Athabasca River winding its way north. Soon the confluence of the Clearwater could be seen at Fort McMurray. Just 86 km to the east was the settlement of Portage La Loche where I had been stationed for over a year. My mind filled with a jumble of memories. It was a difficult place to live and work, never-the-less the experience had been good for me. I remembered with pleasure that this was where I first met Iris, now far away and almost forgotten in the Yukon. We sang the hit songs of the sixties all night with friends at the Hudson's Bay manager's house. It all seemed so long ago. 'At least it wasn't dull there,' I thought to myself. The Conservation Officer was the only Government representative in town, and so the duties varied greatly, ranging from reading the power meters to issuing welfare cheques and providing lumber for coffins. There was even a small tractor and plow used to work gardens. Once in a while I was able to get involved with the trappers and fishermen on various projects. Since almost everyone in the village qualified for social welfare assistance, it was difficult to interest anyone in useful self-help programs. Yes, it had been a tough place, but there was a lot of history there too. I remembered standing on the Methy Portage where the trail went west from Wallis Bay on Methy Lake, across the height-of-land and down to the Clearwater River. On this same ground many adventurers had struggled, pursuing their dreams to the rich fur country of the Athabasca and north to the Beaufort Sea.

Alexander Mackenzie, Peter Pond and many others had toiled over this same muskeg and thrilled to the spectacular beauty spread out below as they reached the east side of the Clearwater Valley. Just being on that famous trade route had left a lasting impression on me. Was the same spirit of adventure that carried so many over that historic portage to the breath-taking splendor of the Clearwater Hills, now drawing me along similar paths?

Life seldom unfolds in reality as we imagine it should, so I was somewhat taken aback when I arrived in Fort Smith and learned that I wouldn't be going to Baker Lake any time soon. Plans apparently changed quite regularly in the Game Management Service and the Superintendent had a new one for me.

The Game Management headquarters occupied an old dwelling house in Fort Smith. The Superintendent was rightfully quartered in what was once the master bedroom, while desks of the other staff were tucked in corners and in the bedrooms upstairs. Maps adorned the walls obscuring the flower-patterned wallpaper.

After a quick tour of the place and much hand shaking, I was back in the boss's office. Paul Kwaterowsky eyed me shrewdly, and in his heavy German accent announced my assignment.

'Well, I think we will send you to Fort Simpson for now. Then we can talk about Baker Lake some other time.'

I tried to remain optimistic about this change in events. I learned that I would be filling in for an officer who was leaving for the summer on educational leave. Well, that wouldn't be forever, and wasn't Fort Simpson sort of the gateway to the legendary Nahanni country? I was beginning to feel better already.

I stood day-dreaming on the banks of the mighty Slave River and listened to the roar of the Rapids Of The Drowned. How many others had stood here before me and gazed out over the surging water with a vision of far away places and high adventure? I would go to Fort Simpson, or anywhere else for that matter, if it helped to ensure that I could see more of this beautiful unspoiled wilderness. Far to the west, across the mysterious Headless Range of mountains, on into the Yukon, was the girl I loved. If it should be that this love was not possible, I knew that this country of pristine beauty would be my mistress, and in its vast expanse, I could forget.

CHAPTER TWO

The Big Rivers

By a thousand dying campfires
Down the rushing rivers wide
They will tell their lonely story
If in them you will confide.

Voyageurs

I ARRIVED IN THE VILLAGE of Fort Simpson in late June. The Javelin turbo-prop thudded down on the rough gravel runway as the stewardess began a verbal routine more suitable to a city airport. 'Please remain in your seats with your seat belts fastened until the aircraft has come to a complete stop in front of the terminal building.' I looked out the window and chuckled. Several vehicles were parked beside a small dilapidated oil shed – the only 'terminal' in sight.

The officer I was replacing for the summer met me with his wife and we began the dusty journey to the village. As we entered the main street his wife insisted that I be treated to a tour. Fort Simpson was a clean, well-planned settlement and I was suitably impressed. 'I'll have no problem spending the summer here,' I thought, as we drove around.

There was a big sign on the river bank just above the dock which stated proudly, 'Welcome to Fort Simpson, The Garden Capital of the North.' I thought the sign a bit odd until I realized that our office was next door to an agricultural experimental station. Behind the shop and warehouse was a small field of barley. Nearby a large greenhouse was full of a great variety of plants. The village was located on a large island in the Mackenzie River and the soil was a rich sandy loam. People grew excellent gardens here, I was told.

In a matter of days I was on my own and anxious to get on the river. The Game Management scow was tied at the dock and I gave it a close inspection. It was eight meters in length and two meters wide, built entirely of plywood and spruce lumber. It was not a pretty craft, with a stub bow and flat bottom, but it looked entirely practical for river travel. It drew

4

less than twenty centimeters of water and was powered by twin 33 hp short-shafted motors. I sat in the scow for a few minutes looking across the broad expanse of the Mackenzie River. Gros Cap, the promontory which marked the confluence of the Liard, shimmered in the afternoon sun several kilometers to the southeast. A warm wind wafted the scent of new vegetation across the water. Out in the surging current innumerable floating logs and woody debris hurried north. The spring flood was bringing its annual delivery of trees from the banks of the Liard. It would be days before the river would be safe to travel. Soon I tired of the warm June sun and the sound of the river and made my way up the bank to the village.

Moise Antoine had lived around Fort Simpson all his life and had worked for the Game Management Service for many years as a patrolman. He had accepted me with tacit indifference as his temporary boss. I hoped I could get through the summer without too much trouble, and that Moise and I could work together.

I heard that a hard liquor outlet was planning to open in town and I wondered what the future would hold for the residents. I had witnessed the disastrous effects wreaked on the people of La Loche and wondered if it would be repeated here. I hoped the liquor store would not create problems for Moise, or others like him.

I had been told that a Big Game Guide training course had been organized for early July at Little Dall Lake in the Mackenzie Mountains. I was looking forward to it. The trainees were to be native lads from the various villages, and it would be necessary to travel around collecting everyone for the course. The big rivers were still running with a full load of wood debris making travel by scow impossible. I decided to pick up the trainee at Trout Lake first since it was necessary to fly in. I went over to see Pete Cowie at Northern Mountain Airways to set up a charter.

Pete was a likable fellow and I asked him about his strange bird tied up at the dock on the river. I had never seen a Found Aircraft before. Pete laughed as he began to extol the virtues of this new airplane. The best way for me to describe it is to say that if it were possible for a Cessna 180 to mate successfully with a Beaver aircraft, the offspring would be the Found. It had the Cessna's nose, the Beaver's door, the Cessna's tail, and so on. Pete reassured me that it was a fine machine, and he arranged the charter for the next morning.

There was enough clear water on the lee side of the island to effect a smooth take-off. As we turned out over the Liard, I was pleased to see the load of debris in the river had begun to subside. We should be able to get on the river in a day or two.

The flight to Trout Lake was uneventful. This large lake is located just north of the Northwest Territories border, and several families with ties to Fort Liard lived there. Dick Turner from Nahanni Butte had operated a trading post here for several seasons before closing.

As we splashed down near the south end of the lake, I was surprised to see sandy beaches and well-built log buildings on the shore. It was a pleasant spot indeed. The residents appeared from their cabins and I was soon engaged in renewing General Hunting Licences and taking care of other overdue administrative matters. Angus Punch, the Big Game Guide Trainee, showed up and we prepared to leave. By suppertime we were tying up the Found aircraft at the dock in Fort Simpson.

The next morning I drove out with Moise on the airport road to have a look at the Liard. There were still numerous rafts of floating wood bobbing along in the main channel, but it was much reduced and the edges were relatively clear. 'What do you think?' I casually posed the question to Moise. He took a long drag on his cigarette as he studied the river. 'Tomorrow'll be okay,' was his laconic reply.

The following day, while most of the village slept, we loaded the scow and set off for Nahanni Butte. Before long we were plowing upstream in the muddy Liard, dodging floating logs and debris. As the clear June morning progressed, long stretches of forested riverbank passed behind us. I will never forget my first trip up the Liard. The wild roses were in full bloom and the aromatic fragrance drifted out over the river to mingle with the scent of spruce needles and new vegetation. Around every bend, the warm zephyrs bore the sweet mixture. I drew it in deeply and all the while my mind absorbed the rugged beauty of the river squeezed between shrub-shrouded banks. Whenever I think of the Liard River, I can still smell the wild roses.

The sun was past the zenith before Moise nosed the scow into the mouth of a creek for a mug-up. After a short rest we were picking our way through the white-water of the Beaver-Dam Rapids. I thought of those who had challenged the indomitable strength of these rivers in small boats. I had heard the story of R. M. Patterson who poled his small canoe to Nahanni Butte on his way up the South Nahanni River to Virginia Falls. Our powerful motors pushed the scow through each surging crest with ease. How different it must have been for Patterson and Faille. They had ample grit to see them through and a real flair for adventure. Albert Faille still lived in Fort Simpson. I passed his cabin daily on my walk to work. I hadn't seen him about. Perhaps even now he was once again testing his mettle against the rivers on yet another trip up the South Nahanni and the Flat.

As the afternoon wore on I could see the shimmering bell-shaped outline of the Butte, still many kilometers to the west on the hazy blue horizon.

Nahanni Butte showing school.

Slinking away to the north was the Nahanni Range of mountains. It was around seven o'clock that evening before we swung the scow out of the muddy Liard and into the clear blue-green waters of the South Nahanni. We beached and tied up just below the log school and teacherage.

Across the river forest-green ridges swept away and upward to meet the massive imposing butte outlined against the clear June sky. I threw down my pack and stood on the bank taking in the beauty of my surroundings. I needed to remember this place just as I was now seeing it, for the first time. Below where I stood on the bank, the South Nahanni River surged and hissed on its way down from those mysterious canyons to the west, anxious, it seemed, to mingle its clear green water with the muddy turbulence of the Liard.

We cooked our evening meal with the Coleman gas stove on the bow of the scow. After we had eaten we sat around drinking tea and watching the river. Some of the native residents dropped by and I renewed their General Hunting Licences. Finally we grabbed our bedrolls and mosquito bars and headed for the one room school. We rolled our sleeping robes out on the floor and strung the mosquito bars between the desks. Soon after I had crawled into my bed I drifted off dreaming of big rivers and beautiful mountains.

CHAPTER THREE

Into the Mountains

I see the face of the mountain
Etched in the clear Arctic sky
The wind in the valley is calling to me
And my heart keeps wondering why?

Eons Of Time

It was late the following day before we left to return to Fort Simpson. The Guide Trainees from Fort Liard had not arrived as planned, so I occupied the morning renewing licences on the school steps. It was a perfect June morning, clear and bright. Occasionally I would glass the green slopes and rocky ridges of the butte looking for Dall's sheep. Finally everyone arrived and we loaded the scow for the trip down-river. The long daylight hours made it possible to travel all night without stopping. We made good time traveling with the spring flood.

Russ Hall, from head office, arrived with his wife on the scheduled flight that afternoon. On the drive in from the airstrip he filled me in on the plans for the training course. A single-engine Otter aircraft on floats had been chartered to fly everything in to Little Dall Lake. I was to go in with the first contingent of trainees and supplies. A young taxidermist from Edmonton was due to arrive the next day and would also go in on the first flight. After we were dropped off at Little Dall Lake, the Otter would fly to Flat Lake, Yukon and pick up a rancher who was part owner of the big game outfitting business that would be operating out of Little Dall Lake, and hopefully hiring some of the Guides we were training. Russ would come in on the last flight from Fort Simpson with the remainder of the supplies. I received verbal directions on how to find the camp after we were dropped at the lake. It was suppose to be five or six kilometers to the southeast. Details were vague, but I did not press the issue as I felt I could find the camp.

It was late afternoon before I was able to gather the supplies and get everyone together and down to the Float Dock. Some of the native lads had been doing some heavy drinking the night before and were suffering

Roasting caribou ribs over an open fire near Little Dall Lake.

severe hang-overs. The Northwest Air Otter had been waiting for some time. Rocky Parsons was the pilot, and the arrival of my motley crew didn't put him in a very good mood. A fight started between two members of the group and the atmosphere on the dock was a bit tense. Rocky was quick to intervene. He brandished a fuel drum wrench in the air and barked loudly, 'If there's any more fighting when you get on my airplane, I'll lay you out cold with this!' His size, the wrench, and his grizzly bear mood had a sobering effect and the aircraft was loaded without further incident.

We cast off the lines and drifted out into the river. Rocky waved me to the co-pilot's seat and fired up the engine. After take-off we followed the Mackenzie River north almost to Wrigley before we turned west toward the mountains. The peaks of the Mackenzie Range loomed on the horizon and before long they were slipping beneath us. We were flying at 9,000 feet altitude and the pilot was navigating his course carefully. I loved to fly, and had received my licence in 1963. I liked to observe other pilots in my attempt to become more proficient. Rocky balanced his map on his knees, periodically taking a sun shot with his astro-compass. I felt quite confident in his flying ability. I was not surprised when we came over Little Dall Lake on course and on time.

We began to circle as we lost altitude, spiraling down to the lake. Soon we were near 1000 feet above terrain. Rocky jabbed a finger at his side window and yelled above the roar of the engine, 'That's the camp right there.' As he turned the aircraft toward the lake I spotted a small wooden building and several tent frames. We were north of the lake and this didn't tie in at all with what Russ had told me. He had said the camp was southeast of the lake.

As we turned on final I looked back at our passengers. They were slumped in their seats, and the ones who had been drinking looked bad. The smell of vomit was in the air; they had obviously been very airsick.

After landing, Rocky taxied to the north shore. We unloaded our gear and supplies on the gravel beach then watched as the Otter took off. Rocky banked in a climbing turn over the lake to gain altitude before setting a course for Flat Lake, Yukon.

I stood looking out over the lake wondering what our next move should be. I had been told to get to the camp and get things set up before the last trip arrived. The pilot had been so sure this was the camp; but why was the location so different from what Russ had described? Someone had it wrong, that was obvious.

I decided I had better walk in and look the camp over first before we did anything else. I checked our gear and the rifle was missing. 'Just great,' I muttered to myself. 'Just great.' I slung the small portable two-way radio on my shoulder and set out. A young lad from Nahanni Butte decided to accompany me. 'No map and no rifle,' I lamented as we started out. I had tried to get a map in Fort Simpson, but since this lake was out of the district there were none available.

It was tough walking through willows, dry creek beds and over loose rock. We arrived at the camp to find everything essential there: tents, pots, pans and dishes. How many camps could there be in these remote mountains? This had to be it.

'We go back now,' I said to my companion who understood very little English.

Our route back took us along a little stream that fed a long narrow lake. We hadn't gone very far when I heard a loud 'Woof' and I knew we had disturbed a bear. 'Don't move! Don't make a sound!' I whispered.

The 'woofing' was now punctuated with grunts and growls as a large grizzly bear stood up on his hind legs less than 200 meters down the slope. He went down on all fours ripping at the tundra with his front feet, swinging his head from side to side. In a matter of seconds he was charging up the slope toward us. 'Don't move,' I repeated. 'We won't have a chance if we run.'

The bear continued the charge toward us but as he got closer his pace slowed and he finally stopped. Again he went through the ritual he had performed further down the slope. He charged a few meters closer, but not quite as fast as before. Again he stopped.

My heart was pounding so loud I felt the bear might hear it. The bear was now less than 75 meters away, looking right at us.

After what seemed like eternity the bear turned and ambled down the slope a short distance. He kept looking back over his shoulder. We hardly dared to breathe. He turned in our direction several times but continued to work his way down-slope to the edge of the stream. To my surprise the bear went into the water and started swimming the short distance to the other side. I began to relax a little. 'I think he's going away,' I said, hopefully.

The bear got out on the far side and went tearing up the bank. 'Let's go!' I said and started walking. We had only gone a short distance when we heard the bear again. He was coming back down the bank. At the water the bear stopped momentarily, then turned and galloped back up the bank, disappearing in the brush.

The trip back through the shrubs and dry creek beds was tense to say the least. 'What if we walk into a sow with cubs?' I thought.

Back at the lake there was a lot of talk in Slavey as the boy from Nahanni Butte told his story. It was getting late so I had to make a decision. 'Get your blankets and whatever grub you can carry. We're walking back to the camp.' I had no intention of sleeping under the stars on this rocky lakeshore.

I managed to find a more direct route this time and soon we had reached the camp and had tents set up and a fire going. Tea and a pot of stew were soon available for my now sober crew.

In the morning I got everyone working; fixing up the camp and hauling the rest of the supplies in from the lake. The young taxidermist spent most of his time fishing in the lake and when he wasn't fishing, he was complaining. He was right out of the city and probably had never camped out in his life.

Around noon I heard the single-engine Otter land on the lake. Everything in camp was in order. Before long, Russ stormed into camp with two native men. He was out of breath and just a little irritated. 'You're in the wrong camp!' he announced.

His attitude irked me. 'You never told me there were two camps,' I said. 'This was the camp according to the pilot; this was where he dropped us off.'

I guess he could see I was really ticked off because he mellowed quickly and said, 'I know, we couldn't get any cooperation from him either.' He didn't elaborate.

'Well,' I said, 'I guess we'll just have to move.'

So move we did. Everyone loaded as much gear as they could carry on their backs and off we went. It was a good eight-kilometer hike across a mountain plateau southeast of the lake to an old mining camp that had been built by the Redstone Mining Company. The tents were bigger and there was a cookshack – definitely more comfortable than the spike-camp we had been in.

Feeling somewhat responsible for the screw-up, I unloaded my pack, had some tea and then said to Russ. 'I'm going back to get another load.' By the time I got back to the spike-camp I was exhausted. I opened a can of fruit and went in the little shack to rest. It wasn't very long before I heard something outside. 'Oh no, not more grizzlies?' I jumped up and peeked out a crack in the door. Then I heard voices. The Indian lads were outside. Apparently they had decided after I left that they should come and give me a hand, although no one had asked them to. I commended them for coming and we began to prepare our packs.

We were all near the end of our physical reserves and we had to stop often to rest. It was hard going over the alpine tundra tussocks. When we reached the trail from the lake things got better. At our rest stops the native boys would spot sheep, caribou or moose on the mountain slopes. I wished I could understand their language, as I listened to their excited conversation. I knew they had a healthy respect for bears, as a result of our earlier experience.

We arrived back at the main camp exhausted. After some supper, we went to the tent. Outside, the young taxidermist was complaining to Russ about how bad everything was. To me, just to be in these beautiful mountains where game abounded on every hillside was an opportunity I was glad I hadn't missed.

The camp lasted a week. I taught First Aid, and once when I was in the middle of a discussion Russ' wife Marg, who was cooking for the camp, came over with blood dripping from her hand. She had gashed it while opening a can and it was bleeding profusely. This was the perfect 'teachable moment' as I demonstrated how to apply pressure to stop the bleeding. After bandaging her hand I picked up the discussion again.

We took the trainees on several field trips. We would pose as the sport hunters and they would guide us to the big game. This gave them some idea what they might expect from actual hunters. On one occasion I took a group up some low mountains early one morning to get some camp meat. We were climbing a steep ridge so we had to rest periodically. I rejoiced at every opportunity to admire the splendor of these mountains. The sun was just lifting the mist from the valley. Directly opposite the ridge we were on, another mountain stood etched against the sky. As we sat quietly, a pack of wolves began to howl on the lower slopes, their cries echoing in the valley. As the mist drifted off, we could see a nursery band of Dall's sheep at about our level, but on the mountain directly across the narrow valley. Some of the ewes were grazing while others were lying down resting with their lambs. It was another of the many scenes I vowed

I would never forget. Later in dreary meetings I would recall these moments and rejoice once again in the misty morning on the ridge when all seemed at perfect peace.

When we topped the summit we spotted a small band of caribou resting on a patch of snow. They scattered as we approached, then stopped to stare curiously several hundred meters away. I dropped a young bull and we were soon occupied in preparing the meat for the trip to camp. We took the head as well. This was used to teach the Guides how to 'cape-out' a trophy.

The week passed quickly – too quickly for my liking. I would have been content to stay on until freeze-up. Soon we were packing our gear back up the trail to the lake. As we waited for the aircraft to arrive for the flight out, we sat on the beach or patrolled the shoreline. One of the native lads had a fishing line in the lake. He didn't seem to be catching much, when suddenly he started yelling something in Slavey. Everyone gathered around to watch. He was pulling on his hand line with great excitement. Either he had caught the bottom of the lake or he had a very large fish on his line.

He began pulling in his line hand over hand and to everyone's amazement the head and back of a very large trout appeared in the shallows. I would have guessed it to be no less than 15 kilograms. The fisherman tried to haul it out on the gravel but it began to thrash about in the shallows and threw the hook. There was great excitement as two of the lads jumped in the water and attempted to catch it with their hands. Fortunately for the fish, it managed to escape. We had a good laugh at the antics, then sat down and continued the wait for the plane.

Eventually the Northwest Air single-engine Otter arrived and taxied in to shore. I noticed that we had a different pilot and I wished that it was Rocky Parsons climbing out on the float instead of someone I didn't know. At least I had confidence in Rocky's flying ability. The weather was marginal and I couldn't help wishing that we would wait for it to improve. The 'crud-type' clouds were below the mountain peaks and visibility wasn't that great. I had heard all the gory details of a crash that had taken place 16 km from this very lake the previous October. Bill Berg from Fort Simpson was starting up an outfitting business and was making the last trip out for the season with three guides in marginal conditions when they crashed and burned on a mountain slope. Ironically the Beaver belonged to Northern Mountain Airways in Fort Simpson, and was the same aircraft (registration CF-IOB) that Bob Gauchie had spent 58 days surviving in on Samandre Lake before he was found and rescued. The thought of this accident had a sobering effect on me as I glanced up at the low cloud hanging over the lake.

The first flight was to take Daryl over to Flat Lake. Daryl asked me if

I wanted to go with him to see the country. I opened my mouth to say no, but instead I heard myself say, 'Sure, why not?' The 'why not' should have been painfully obvious but it was almost impossible for me to refuse a plane ride over new country. The plan was to fly to Flat Lake, drop Daryl off, then return and pick up the crew for the trip to Fort Simpson.

We were no sooner airborne when I wished intensely that I had stayed at the lake. We began following the Redstone River valley southwest after lifting off the lake. The ceiling got lower as the flight progressed. Only the slopes of the mountains were visible on either side of the valley. A steep banking turn alerted me of trouble and I cinched my seatbelt a notch tighter. Daryl was sitting up front in the co-pilot's seat. I was sitting in the first seat in the cabin. Out my window all that was visible was ragged, wisps of cloud and beyond, the rugged slope of a mountain.

The pilot was trying to fly visual and apparently had strayed too close to the edge of the valley. He tried to pick up his course again, and I began to wonder if he had ever flown these mountain passes before. I felt sure we were going to crash if we kept stumbling around in this valley.

I yelled, 'Daryl, Daryl!' at the top of my lungs.

Finally he glanced back.

'Tell him to get us back to the lake!'

Daryl's face was as pale as chalk but he nodded in the affirmative. Before he could get the pilot's attention we were suddenly in a steep turn to the left. I glanced forward and could see a rocky slope off to the right. 'This is it,' I thought. 'We've been suckered into a blind canyon.' As we were completing the turn I looked out the port window and watched the wingtip pass over a ridge not more than 100 meters below. If a downdraft had grabbed us at that moment it would have been over for us. I heard Daryl yelling at the pilot. The turn was extended to 180 degrees and at last we were heading back up the valley toward the lake. I took a deep breath and prayed that the weather had not closed in behind us. Somehow we managed it and the sweetest of sounds was the water kissing the floats as we touched the lake.

The weather improved slightly as the day went on, but the trip to Flat Lake was scrapped. When we felt the weather had improved and we could see the tops of the mountains again, we loaded the plane and headed for Fort Simpson. Everyone was tense and nervous until we cleared the mountains and could see the Mackenzie River.

As we left the beautiful Mackenzie Mountains behind, I reviewed the memories of the past week in my mind and vowed I would return if I ever got another chance. I thought of Daryl back at the camp. He would have to wait there until the weather improved and another charter could be arranged. Somehow it was difficult to feel sorry for him.

CHAPTER FOUR

Across Great Bear Lake

Oh take a journey northward
Through a bright and shining land
That has a special blessing
Given by God's wondrous hand.

Northern Journey

AFTER THE TRAINING CAMP in the mountains, life at Fort Simpson became dismally routine. The mail strike was over and I finally received a letter from Iris in Whitehorse. She seemed interested in where I was and what I had been doing. As I prepared a reply I couldn't help wondering if we still had a future together.

As July faded and August arrived, I began to wonder when I would receive word on my move to Baker Lake. Perhaps I should just forget about it. I had picked up a rumour that Hugh, the officer I was replacing, would be moving up to a headquarters position after he returned from educational leave. There was a chance I would be able to stay on in Fort Simpson.

'Why would you want to go to a god-forsaken place like Baker Lake anyway?' Bernie Gauchier asked one afternoon over tea. He was the Forest Officer with the Mackenzie Land and Forest Service and we shared the same office building. I didn't have an immediate reply. Baker Lake seemed further away with each passing day. I mumbled something about wanting to see the Arctic as I tried to change the subject.

A message came through on the Forestry radio that brought relief to the daily tedium. Russ Hall from headquarters was coming in on the scheduled flight and asked me to meet the plane. Perhaps he would bring some news about my future.

Russ and his wife Marg got off the one o'clock flight. On the drive back to the settlement he outlined the purpose of the trip. Word had been received at headquarters that the Arctic Circle Lodge on Great Bear Lake was serving wild meat to patrons. The information indicated that the meat

15

had been taken illegally and there was plenty of it in the freezers. The plan was to charter Pete Cowie and his Found, fly up to Great Bear and investigate the matter. A similar investigation awaited us across the lake near Hornby Bay where a mining camp was operating.

Early next morning we lifted off the river and headed north. We made one stop en route at Willowlake River where I was able to clear up some administrative problems. As the flight went on to Fort Franklin I reflected on the diverse beauty of the uninhabited landscape that seemed to stretch forever before us. I yearned to view new country and so far that wish was being fulfilled completely.

The day was well advanced as we drew near Fort Franklin on the Keith Arm of Great Bear Lake. As we crossed the extreme southwestern tip I could see that there was still a lot of ice in the big lake. It was too late in the day to proceed further so we sought accommodation in an empty staff house in the settlement.

The good flying weather held, and early next morning we headed east, out over the Great Bear, keeping the north shore in sight. Looking through the windscreen straight ahead was like looking at the Atlantic Ocean: water as far as the eye could see. The Found hummed along high above the water. Turning north we spotted the Arctic Circle Lodge tucked into a protective bay on the north shore. The floats touched the surface ripple gently and we headed to the dock.

The owner/manager greeted us with a big handshake and a friendly line of chit-chat. Obviously, he didn't know the purpose of our mission. We were invited in and over coffee we diplomatically explained why we were there. He seemed surprised, but no less friendly. He claimed absolutely no knowledge of any game meat in his freezers, but invited us to look for ourselves.

The lodge was very large and posh. In the kitchen, a chef in whites went about his business. In the first freezer we found meat wrapped and marked. We were surprised to find packages marked 'ptarmigan', 'caribou' and 'moose'. The manager claimed that the meat must have been there a long time and that none of it had ever been served to patrons. There was no way of proving one way or the other if it was legally taken game or not. Since there were native guides working for the lodge, it was possible that they could claim the meat. There was no evidence of any of the meat being cooked or served in the lodge. We seized samples of the meat for evidence in case charges were to be considered. After taking statements from pertinent people, we concluded the investigation.

The manager, in true northern fashion, insisted that we have dinner at the lodge before we left. I felt we were compromising our position somewhat by accepting a meal, but the long flight over the lake had left us very hungry. With the aroma of food wafting through the dining room, the temptation was just too great. The finest hotel in the south could not have provided better fare. We dined sumptuously unnoticed by the other lodge guests.

Soon we were winging our way east again. We had now travelled over 200 km from the Keith Arm to the Dease Arm of the lake. It would be another 160 km to McTavish Arm and Hornby Bay. The whole lake was about 280 km in length, I estimated from our maps; undoubtedly one of the world's great lakes. The Found continued to throb smoothly putting the huge expanse of water behind us. Hornby Bay appeared on the horizon and soon we were circling the mining camp near the mouth of the Sloan River. It was late afternoon and only the cook was in the camp. He was able to provide us with the information we required and once again we were airborne across McTavish Arm to Sawmill Bay.

We landed at the fishing lodge and Pete refuelled the aircraft. It was now past midnight so we rested for several hours to time our arrival back in Fort Simpson in daylight. The 448 km flight home was lengthy and tedious. I was sitting up front with the pilot; Russ and his wife were sitting in the back. After the first hour everyone became very sleepy. It had been a long day. I could see that Pete was fighting to stay awake. He fiddled with the radio, shuffled and reshuffled his maps and checked his logbook. I didn't want to discourage his efforts by falling asleep myself. It was a tough fight. The engine vibration was most conducive to sleep. Once or twice I nodded off briefly. I think Pete must have dozed also. Russ was sound asleep in the back seat, but I noticed Marg was wide-eyed staring forward. She told me later that she was just a little shook up when she glanced forward once and noticed Pete and me both dozing.

The flight continued without incident and the eastern sky began to lighten, painting the scattered cloud with golden hues as we neared Willowlake River. The sun had just cleared the horizon as we splashed down on the Mackenzie River; home once more to Fort Simpson.

CHAPTER FIVE

Up the Liard in Style

Upon a mighty river
Flowing to the rising sun
It is the very finest of all other ones.

Northern Journey

ONE DROWSY FRIDAY AFTERNOON my phone jangled to life. A clerk at Headquarters was on the line telling me Norman Simmons, a Canadian Wildlife Service Biologist, was en route from Fort Smith in a jet boat. He was doing a field study of Dall's sheep in the Mackenzie Mountains and might need support and assistance. I should expect him to contact me when he arrived in Fort Simpson. He might need a guide to take him up to Dead Man's Valley. I said I would do what I could to help.

After I hung up the phone I headed out to the shop/warehouse to catch Moise before he left work. He was tinkering with one of the outboard motors. I asked him if he would mind taking a biologist up-river if he needed a guide. Moise said he could.

'You weren't planning to go anywhere over the week-end, were you?'

'No, I'll be around,' was his reply.

'That's good,' I countered. 'Because he's coming in on the week-end and might want to get an early start Monday morning.'

Moise grunted acknowledgement. 'Well, we'll see you on Monday then,' I concluded hopefully, as I headed back to the office.

My lingering apprehension concerning Moise was confirmed Sunday morning when I heard a knock at the door. I opened to find one of Moise's little boys standing outside.

'Moise wants to see you,' he said with some hesitancy.

'Why can't he come here?' I asked, expecting bad news.

'He's in the hospital,' was the little boy's reply as he turned to go.

As I walked toward the hospital I had a premonition that alcohol would be involved. The nurse escorted me to his bedside. Moise opened his eyes as I approached.

18

'What happened?' I asked simply.

Moise avoided my question. His face was swollen and he looked a real mess.

'I'm hurt bad,' he said. 'Maybe my ribs broken.'

'What happened?' I repeated.

'Some guys beat me real bad,' Moise groaned.

After I had determined that his injuries were not life threatening I wished him a speedy recovery and left. I knew he wouldn't be able to work for quite a while.

It didn't take me long to get the full story. Poor Moise had been in the 'sauce' and had made some violent enemies. They came to his house late at night, broke in, and pounded him up.

I remembered this was a regular occurrence in La Loche. Arms and even legs were sometimes broken, and everything in the house smashed. It looked like Moise had been lucky as his arms and legs were still intact. 'Demon' liquor and an apparent inability to drink moderately was usually the reason for this kind of misery.

This of course left me without a patrolman to help the biologist. On Sunday afternoon Norman Simmons arrived from Fort Smith in a brand new jet boat. As I headed down the riverbank where he had beached the boat, I met his wife Hilah coming up the bank with a blond-haired little girl in one hand and a large husky dog on a chain in the other. The family was planning to fly in to Dead Man's Valley after Norm got up there with the jet boat.

I reluctantly informed Norm of the condition of my patrolman. He appeared disappointed. He said he had been hoping for an early start on Monday. As we mulled things over, Norm introduced me to his helmsman, a young man who lived in Fort Norman. I learned that he had handled boats on the Keele River. I didn't think they would have much trouble if he had been on the Keele, but Norm said the new jet boat had yet to be tested in white-water and he had hoped someone could come along who knew the river.

'Well,' I said, 'I'll be glad to take you up to Nahanni Butte. You can probably find someone to take you on from there.'

Norm agreed, and plans were set for an early morning departure. I phoned Northern Mountain Airways and arranged for a charter to pick me up in Nahanni Butte.

Once again I was on my way up the Liard, this time in style. The new jet boat was an eight-meter aluminium beauty powered by a big Ford industrial engine. It made the old Game Management scow look like a rowboat. In white-water it handled like a dream. The track through the rapids on the Liard was still fresh in my mind and we skimmed through with little effort. This was surely the outfit for river travel. We covered 184 km against the current to Nahanni Butte in ten hours.

We made supper in the log house assigned as a teacherage but currently unoccupied. Norm planned to go across the river to meet Dick Turner. He needed as much information as he could get before tackling the South Nahanni. The sound of the Ford motor brought Dick Turner out of his comfortable log home and down to the shore. He cast an appraising eye over the new jet boat as Norm introduced himself and us. Dick greeted us warmly and invited us up to the house. As we stepped inside Dick introduced his wife Vera and Albert Faille. As Albert shook my hand, I noticed how difficult it was for him to stand erect. That stooped frame told much of the hard years he had spent on the rivers and in the bush. His grasp was firm however; and his keen eyes met mine as we exchanged greetings.

Over steaming cups of tea, Dick and Albert began to review the route up the South Nahanni much like farmers would describe their 'back 40'. Norm was taking notes and asking questions. Dick figured the tricky part would be in choosing the right channel to follow through the 'splits' as the current caused seasonal changes. 'If you find you picked the wrong one, don't get excited, just go back and try a different one.' There was some talk of a young American who was on the river with a canoe. Apparently he had made it to the second canyon, which was considered an achievement considering the fact that he was alone and didn't know the river. 'Maybe he's another draft dodger,' someone remarked.

Dick walked back to the jet boat with us. 'You shouldn't have any trouble on the Nahanni with an outfit like that,' he commented to Norm as we pushed off.

Next morning my plane arrived and I left Nahanni Butte for the last time. I'm glad I only saw it as a small village, remote and beautiful. After a short visit to Fort Liard to pick up some fur returns, I flew back to Fort Simpson.

CHAPTER SIX

Caribou Hunt

I remembered the tent on a gravel ridge
And the caribou breaking the hill.
The Northern Lights on a placid lake
When the cold wind, at last, is still.

Home to the Northland

THE MIDDLE OF AUGUST arrived and I still didn't know when or if I would be going to Baker Lake. Yellowknife had recently been selected as the capital of the Northwest Territories, and our office was in the process of moving. Perhaps they would forget about me altogether or ask me to stay on in Fort Simpson.

I received another letter from Iris in Whitehorse. She sounded lonely and as unsure of the future as I. She discussed what was happening generally, but in my reply I avoided making commitments or asking too many questions. In time we would know how things were meant to be. We still expressed sincere affection in our letters, but we had been separated too long for the words to have much meaning.

A summons finally arrived to go to Yellowknife on the next scheduled flight. I breathed a great sigh of relief and began to gather my things. Once again I was sitting in front of the Superintendent of Game's desk: a new desk in a new office. Paul was the same and still puffed on his ubiquitous cigar, but everything else had changed. The new Territorial Government Bureaucracy had moved from Ottawa and there was a whole new empire to build in Yellowknife.

'Well, do you still want to go to Baker Lake, or would you be happier here in the west?' Paul's accented voice brought me back from my admiring glances about the new office. I had asked myself this very question several times over the summer and had always answered with a clear 'Yes, you bet I do!' Now suddenly I wasn't so sure. The last letter I had received from Iris had set me thinking. Did I really want to go so far away? Would this move be the 'death knell' of our relationship? Paul's voice interrupted my hesitation.

'Anyway, I want you to go on a caribou hunt.' He took the cigar from his mouth, inspecting it intently as he rolled it in his fingers. 'Some Indians from Fort Rae are hunting north of here. We need some skins, also I have someone I want you to take along.'

What followed was a verbal introduction to Hans Misner, a tourist from Germany who was travelling around gathering material for a book he intended to write about the Northwest Territories.

After the discussion with the Superintendent I headed down to the Game Office on Latham Island to prepare for the trip. I decided this would be an excellent opportunity to put some of my technical training to good use. I would collect as much information on the caribou as I could. Perhaps this would make the 'baby-sitting' part of the trip a little less onerous. Larry Skov patiently went about the warehouse gathering up the equipment I would need.

Mid morning of 21 August found me strolling impatiently around the Float Base waiting for the Superintendent and Hans Misner to arrive. A Beechcraft 18 on floats had been chartered and was loaded and ready to go. Eventually they arrived and we were soon on our way north. En route we checked the area around Snare Lake for caribou or hunters but saw nothing. We continued an irregular course northeast and near Rawalpindi Lake spotted a large hunting encampment. We circled low over the water and landed. The tents were on the edge of a large esker on the north-eastern shore. Meat hung drying on ropes strung between willow posts looking like so much dirty laundry from a distance. Only an older man and some boys were in camp; the rest were out hunting.

We paddled the Beechcraft in to the gravel shore and unloaded. After a few words concerning the pick-up date, we pushed the plane into the lake. I stood with Hans Misner and watched the aircraft roar across the lake, climb steadily and vanish in the southern horizon. 'This should be an interesting week,' I mused as I set about finding a place to pitch the tent.

As I walked along the gravel ridge I was enthralled with the beauty of the fall colors just beginning to touch the shrubbery. This was the first time I had set foot on real tundra, an experience I had thought would take place in Baker Lake. 'Well I'm getting a little closer,' I thought. 'At least I'm near the same latitude.'

After I had the tent up and the camp arranged I went over to the Indian camp and left word that I wanted to buy caribou skins at $5.00 each. Normally they would not keep the skins. When I returned to the tent I found Hans Misner with his rifle about to go hunting. He had recruited one of the young native lads to guide him. I knew he wasn't suppose to be hunting at all because he was a non-resident alien as far as the Game

Author's tent on esker near Dene Camp, Rawalpindi Lake.

Ordinance was concerned. The Superintendent knew this as well as I; so why did he allow him to bring a firearm? I was somewhat irritated at being put in this difficult position, but what could I do?

It became obvious shortly after I arrived that too many caribou had already been shot. Parts of carcasses were lying all over the tundra abandoned. The Indians understandably took those parts of the carcass most conducive to sun-drying. Many kilometers of tough paddling and twenty-three portages stood between this camp and their homes in Fort Rae. The only meat they could take was dry meat. I knew there would be some wastage; but I also knew that by offering to buy hides, I was in fact making matters worse. I appeased my conscience a little by promising to take as much fresh meat back for them as I could when the plane returned.

Hans returned from his hunt and announced curtly that he had shot a caribou and the Indians could go get it if they wanted it. His rather arrogant attitude left me struggling to control my temper. All the Indian hunters were away from camp, so I asked the young Indian boy who had gone with Misner how far away the caribou was. He said, 'Not far,' then informed me that the caribou wasn't dead – only wounded. I knew I had to get away before I lost my temper completely, so I asked the lad if he would take me to it. He agreed and we left immediately. The boy took me to the area where the animal had been shot, but it was nowhere in sight. The boy left to return to his camp and I began searching for a blood trail or some other indication of where the wounded caribou had gone. I went on some distance when suddenly a caribou bolted from behind some rocks in front of me. It was a yearling and I knew the wounded female was close by. It tried to get to its feet when I located it and I finished it off, skinned and gutted it. I had a tump-line strap and rope with me, so I quartered the animal and packed the hind quarters back to our tent. Hans must have guessed that I was less than pleased with him. He left for a walk as soon as I arrived.

Fortunately because it was an average sized female I managed to get the meat to camp in two trips. Later that evening when I had cooled down somewhat, I offered Hans some tea which he accepted. While we were sitting outside the tent I told him that he should refrain from further hunting because he didn't have a licence and that far too much meat was being wasted. He said little in reply but his rifle remained in the tent for the duration of our stay.

I occupied my time roaming the area northeast of the camp where most of the hunting was taking place. I was sickened by the amount of edible meat that was being left to rot. As I located each kill I identified the sex of the animal, collected the mandible for ageing and checked the lungs and liver for disease.

The days passed pleasantly as I wandered almost aimlessly at times over the rise and fall of the colorful landscape. The winds of late August played through generous patches of Labrador tea and dwarf birch, rustling the red and yellow leaves. Cranberry and bearberry added a further splash of color to the mosaic. Periodically small bands of caribou drifted through retracing age-old routes on their restless seasonal migrations. The bulls' antlers were still in velvet giving them a massive top-heavy appearance. Often I simply stopped and gaped in awe at the panorama of life parading before me. The sheer vast purity of the rolling tundra, dotted by countless small lakes and tundra ponds, etched an indelible imprint on my soul. My dream to survey the Arctic was forcefully rekindled and all lingering doubts dispelled.

Some evenings I would join the circle around the fire in the Indian camp. All the hunters were there discussing the day's hunt, conversing in Dogrib, the language of their birth. I noticed the similarity of the words to Chipewyan which I had listened to for a year at La Loche. The boys that spoke English would translate for me when necessary, but I rarely felt the need to converse. Sharing meat and tea and a place by the fire with these carefree hunters was for me sufficient.

I spent the rest of the time with Hans Misner listening patiently to his many stories about his days as a 'diplomatic attaché' in London, England, just before the Second World War. One evening he described his time in prison after the war. His internment was extremely difficult and uncomfortable at first but after a short time the wardenship changed and an American officer was put in charge. He and the others prisoners expected much worse treatment. The American warden called an assembly of all prisoners. Hans said everyone was apprehensive. The warden said he had received no special instructions on how to run the prison, so he intended to run it as he had a prison back in the United States. Hans laughed and said, 'Everything got much better after that, the food, everything! We could hardly believe it.'

I didn't enjoy his tales about the war and resented him somewhat for talking about it but I didn't think it wise for me to be rude so I said nothing. My older brother had been killed in Belgium during the war when he was but a boy of nineteen and I guess I still harboured some resentment toward people such as Hans.

Hans was preoccupied with choosing a title for the book he would write about the Northwest Territories. He was unflattering in his remarks about some of the other Game Officers, most of whom I had not yet had the opportunity to meet. He mentioned Cliff Cook, the Game Officer in Aklavik, in particular. Hans had taken a trip on the Delta with him. He referred to Cliff's 'loud, obscene body noises' and I gathered that this had not been one of his better trips. I kept silent, laughing inwardly at the story. In the confines of a tent this could indeed be quite objectionable to someone like Hans.

I purchased 216 caribou hides for the Government and in so doing probably contributed to the wastage of edible meat which was very much in evidence when I arrived. I intended to write a full report when I returned.

Around 10:30 on the morning of 27 August a single-engine Otter arrived to pick us up. After our gear and hides were loaded, I took on as much meat as the aircraft could carry. The hunters were grateful. By early afternoon I was unloading the plane in Yellowknife.

CHAPTER SEVEN

A Bend in the Trail

Across this sea of snow
Straight home to my love I'll go
Mush along my huskies take me home.

Mush Along

AFTER I RETURNED to Yellowknife I arranged another meeting with the Superintendent. He seemed anxious to know if there had been any problems with Hans Misner. I was sufficiently intimidated by the formality of being in the boss's office that all my comments about him were positive. Fortunately he didn't ask if Hans had killed any caribou. Eventually he turned to the matter of my posting to Baker Lake. I informed him that I wanted to go and was prepared to leave as soon as possible. Paul frowned as he took gentle puffs from his cigar and removed it from his lips.

'Well, I hope you're sure,' he said slowly. 'What about your girlfriend; what does she think?'

This question made me uncomfortable but I answered without hesitation, 'She won't mind.'

'Maybe you should go see her before you go to Baker Lake?'

This suggestion surprised me, though I realized it was an idea I had considered, albeit fleetingly. Somehow hearing it from the Superintendent reinforced the thought. Before I could reply Paul added, 'You must have some days coming from this summer; why don't you go see her?'

I assured him I would seriously consider it and stood up to leave. His secretary appeared at this point and informed me that all the flights were booked out of Yellowknife for the next several days. Yellowknife was bursting at the seams. I had been unable to get a room anywhere in town when I returned from the caribou hunt and had stayed with Art Look, the Game Officer in Yellowknife.

While I sat considering what to do, Paul picked up the phone and made some calls. In a few minutes he announced that I was booked on a 2 a.m.

flight to Edmonton. This was an extra section and somehow he had managed to squeeze me in.

'It must be nice to have that kind of pull,' I thought as I was leaving.

As I winged south in the early hours of the next day, I kicked the idea of visiting Iris around in my mind. Perhaps I should go; it would be one way of sorting out our future. On the other hand maybe it was best just to let our relationship continue the slow death of the last six months. The end couldn't be very far away. I didn't want to continue the letters. Each one was becoming more difficult to write. One minute I was sure of the course I should take and in the next, I was wavering.

We arrived around 5 a.m. and after I had retrieved my luggage I began wandering around the airport in my attempt to reach a decision. The flight to Whitehorse left at 7:30 a.m. Reluctantly I made my way to the Air Canada counter to purchase a ticket to Winnipeg. 'I'll just leave everything as it is,' I whispered to myself as I walked along.

When I got to the ticket counter I had another moment of indecision and instead of approaching the agent, I found a seat and sat down. Iris wouldn't be expecting me, perhaps I should phone first. If I just went up to Whitehorse and things didn't work out, I could take a few days and see a bit of the Yukon before heading to Baker Lake. Thoughts were mush in my tired brain.

I stood up and grabbed my gear. 'I'm going to Whitehorse,' I said firmly and headed toward the Canadian Pacific ticket counter. In a matter of minutes I had a return ticket and a boarding pass in my hand and I sat down to await the flight. 'Something has kept us communicating all these long months. I have to see if we still feel the way we did at the beginning. I can't just walk away. I have to know for sure.'

At the Whitehorse airport I rented a car and drove downtown. My head was filled with a fusion of conflicting thoughts and emotions. I passed a supermarket and pulled into the parking lot. All the apprehension and insecurity I had felt earlier swept over me again like a wave. 'I should have phoned from Edmonton,' I thought. 'But then, isn't this how you usually operate?' I got out of the car and went inside to find a phone.

The market was a clatter of noise from busy shoppers. I found a pay phone and dialled the number for the Nurses' Residence. A female voice answered and when I asked to speak with Iris, said, 'I'll have to go see if she's in.' I felt pressure pounding in my ears as I waited. I started to hang up, then stopped myself. I heard a slight crackle as the receiver was picked up.

'Hello?' It was Iris' voice.

'Hello,' I replied.

'Who's this?'

'It's Ellis.'

There was a long pause.

'Ellis?'

Another pause.

'Is that really you?'

'It's me alright.'

'Where are you?'

'I'm at a supermarket; I don't know the name.'

'Where?'

'I'm at a supermarket. I'm here in Whitehorse.' I was beginning to feel a little foolish.

'You're here in Whitehorse? You're here right now? If you're lying to me I'll kill you!' Her voice was warm and excited.

'I'm really here alright. When can I come to see you?'

'You'd better come right now!'

And so began our renewed romance. I found the Nurses' Residence and parked the car. As I was walking toward the entrance I saw the door open and Iris came running out. I ran to meet her and swept her into my arms. Nothing had changed. The love was still there, stronger than ever.

In the days that followed we became engaged and spent long hours discussing our future together. She was keen for adventure and not daunted at all at the prospect of living in Baker Lake. We toured the attractions, spent an afternoon in Miles Canyon and drove to Haines Alaska. We pledged anew our love and said good-bye as I waited to board the plane for Edmonton.

I trekked on to Winnipeg and north to Churchill. 5 September found me lodged in the sleazy Hudson Hotel waiting for a plane to Baker Lake. The Transair agent seemed unsure about a flight but optimistically advised me to keep in touch. The delay didn't cause me much concern, I knew I would get there eventually and that was all that mattered. I spent some time walking around the town and along the stark shores of Hudson Bay.

A little excitement occurred around 2 a.m. when the door to my hotel room opened and a stranger entered, put his suitcase down and threw his coat on the cot next to mine. I sat up and exclaimed, 'Who might you be and what are you doing in my room?'

The young man apologized for waking me then introduced himself.

'I just got in from Rankin Inlet. The desk clerk said there was an extra bed here – the rest of the hotel's full.'

'Oh,' I replied. 'Well, make yourself at home. How's everything in Rankin these days?'

'I was just there for the summer on construction,' my new roommate replied. 'It wasn't that bad but I'm glad to be heading home.' He began to prepare for bed.

'Where are you heading?'

'Baker Lake,' I replied and rolled over. It took a long time to get back to sleep.

CHAPTER EIGHT

Baker Lake at Last

I've seen the glow of the Arctic sun
As it hangs on the southern brim
Gracing the dark of the Arctic night
With a halo pale and dim.

Home To The Northland

WHEN I PHONED TRANSAIR on Friday, 6 September, the agent cheerfully informed me that there would be a flight at 10 a.m.

'This is your lucky day,' he quipped. 'We weren't planning any flights north until next Tuesday.'

I learned more about my good fortune when I checked in at the airport. A cluster of people milled about toting cameras, binoculars, and knapsacks on their shoulders. One lady stood out as the apparent leader and seemed to be briefing the group. The agent took my ticket and announced seriously, 'This isn't a scheduled flight. That lady over there,' he nodded in the leader's direction, 'she's the wife of the company president.' He began hauling my luggage under the counter.

'They'll be stopping at all the settlements on the way to watch birds.' He straightened up and added with a smile. 'You'll get to Baker Lake sometime today.'

'I sure hope so,' I replied and went over to find a seat where I could study the 'birders' more closely.

Before long we were walking toward an old tired-looking Dakota aircraft. As I waited my turn to board I wondered if they had rolled out the 'Queen of the Fleet' for the president's wife. We flew north straight off the end of the runway out over the white-capped water of Hudson Bay. There was some scattered high cloud but the wind was moderate; a great day for flying. Off to the west the coastline stood out in stark contrast to the dark blue water of the Bay. As the flight progressed we drew closer to land and soon the narrow peninsula on which the village of Eskimo Point was located lay dead ahead. (Today it bears the more politically correct name of Arviat.)

We bounced down the undulant gravel runway, which seemed a bit short. We turned around at the very west end and taxied back toward the village. A few of the Inuit residents showed up, stayed around for awhile, and then departed. The bird-watchers gathered their equipment and headed off in a group toward the nearest tundra pond. Soon only the Pilot, Second Officer and myself were strolling around on the runway near the plane.

Eventually I wandered out on the tundra to look at the vegetation. I marveled at the tiny plants which survived inches from the surface. Labrador tea, which in northern Saskatchewan grew waist high, here ventured mere inches upward. All the plants and shrubs appeared considerably less luxuriant than those I had seen on the tundra north of Yellowknife. I returned to the aircraft and sat around visiting with the pilots. After several hours the group returned.

The take-off run was rough but soon we were airborne and continued cruising north along the coast to Rankin Inlet. Eskimo Point had struck me as a flat dismal place and I was glad I wasn't being posted there. As I gazed down at Rankin Inlet I had a more favorable impression. It seemed like an interesting community. A large mine head frame was the prominent feature. As we circled to land I wondered how Baker Lake would stack up against these coastal communities. The landing was smoother and the runway longer.

The bird-watchers boarded a van and headed to town. We waited around for an hour before the pilots decided to walk down to the village. I joined them and we were able to find a place where we could get some coffee. We met some interesting people at the coffee shop; everyone was friendly and ready to engage in conversation. It was almost 5 p.m. before everyone was back at the plane ready to go.

On the last leg to Baker Lake we flew inland over innumerable lakes, rivers and shallow tundra ponds. Rocky outcropping protruded from the land and long snaking eskers could be seen between the lakes. The vastness of this uninhabited country impressed me greatly. Would I be able to learn the skills necessary to travel and survive in this endless treeless landscape?

We were flying northwest. A very large body of water could be seen ahead of us. This should be Baker Lake. We crossed over the mouth of the Thelon River and turned toward the airstrip that stretched along the east slope of a large flat-topped hill. I could see the settlement hugging the northwest corner of the lake. I pressed my face to the window attempting to get a better view of the village. It appeared small but neatly laid out along the shore.

'I think we'll be able to make a home here.' I thought as the plane banked on final to the airstrip.

A yellow four-wheel-drive station wagon was waiting to meet the plane. A man in a blue parka stood beside it. More vehicles arrived and we began to sort out the luggage. I asked the fellow in the blue parka if he was with Northern Affairs.

'Sure am,' he said. 'I'm Gerry Tanner.'

I shook his outstretched hand and introduced myself.

'Well, glad to meet you at last. We've been expecting you since July!'

'Really?' I responded. 'Well, that's a long story.'

'Yeah, I thought it might be. Well, get your stuff, I'll take you in.'

On the bumpy ride to the community Gerry chatted about what I should expect.

'I hate to tell you this, but the house assigned to you isn't available yet.'

'Oh. Good job I didn't rush up here in July then.'

Gerry laughed. 'They're building two new apartments for the teachers, but it'll be another two weeks before they're ready. There's a teacher living in your place right now.'

Before I had time to reply he added, 'You can stay with me until then if you want to.'

Not knowing what else to say, I accepted his offer.

'I hope I won't be putting you out too much.'

'Not at all,' Gerry replied. 'I hope you won't mind sleeping on the sofa.'

Actually the sofa proved too short and narrow, so I rolled my bedroll out on the living room carpet. I appreciated the generosity of Gerry and his wife Sheena. They had three children and the house was not large. The roof leaked badly as I was to discover the next day when it began to rain. Sheena arranged her cooking pots around the living room to catch the drips. That night I was lulled to sleep by the claphoney of drops as they hit the various sized pots; each with a distinct note.

Most of the Game Management equipment had either disappeared or was in a dismal state of disrepair. There was an office assigned in the Northern Affairs administration building, and most of the forms and records were still there. I began the laborious task of sorting out the files and bringing the licence returns up to date.

Wally Thom was a Game Officer in Aklavik when he was transferred to Baker Lake in 1967. He was only at his new posting for a few months when he was drowned in an aircraft 'tip-over' in front of the village on 28 September. His body was never recovered.

What was so tragic about Wally's death was that it probably could have been avoided. He was going on annual leave and was booked on Transair, the scheduled airline, but managed to talk his way into an empty seat on

Settlement of Baker Lake. Canoes on ice.

a Cessna 180 floatplane that had arrived to fly some contractors south via Uranium City.

It was a cold windy morning when they taxied out on the lake for take-off. Offshore the plane began to turn toward the settlement into the stiff north wind. A gust caught the wing as the plane slipped down in a wave-trough and it began a slow rollover. There was time for the passengers and pilot to get out and cling to the floats. The water was near the freezing point. For some reason, which no one could figure out, Wally jumped clear of the floats. He was a strong swimmer, but no one swims for long in super-cooled water. His last words were 'Throw me my coat, I'm cold.' Seconds later he slipped beneath the choppy water of Baker Lake. Within minutes canoes arrived to rescue the people on the floats. Luckily some people on shore had viewed the accident.

Biologists had frequented Baker Lake during the summer months to study the caribou, beginning in 1949. The Inuit had watched many come and go over the years. No one had taken the time to explain to the people of the country what they were trying to accomplish. The hunters had a vague idea that these summer migrants who were so interested in studying their 'life-blood', the *tuktu*, meant no harm. They did not clearly understand why the biologists had to catch the animals at the water crossings and put metal tags in their ears. The Inuit must have laughed when they learned the *Qallunaaq* (white person) scientists were attempting to count the caribou, a task in their minds comparable to counting the rocks on the tundra, or the stars in the heavens, but they generously accepted them, and began calling them *tuktuluree*, the man who looks after the caribou. I inherited this name when I arrived. It was a logical name; *tuktu* had meant life or death for these inland people for centuries. I vowed to make myself worthy of the name, and place the good management of the caribou at the top of my priority list.

Hugh Ungungai came to the office shortly after I arrived. He had been Wally's Inuit assistant and he indicated that he would like to work for *Tuktuluree*. He found his job as interpreter for the office staff boring and he was hoping for a change. He was amiable, good-natured and spoke English fluently. I told him that it would take some time to clear the office backlog before I would need assistance. Hugh had little information concerning Game Management equipment. Some had been left out on the land. The Skidoo snowmobile was a shell, stripped for parts, and other than the Bombardier snowmobile, little was left; I would have to begin replacing the inventory once again and in the meantime, rent or borrow what I would need to travel on the land.

The arrival of Iris' trunk on a Transair flight reminded me that I had more than work related concerns. We had decided to be married in Baker Lake shortly after she arrived at the end of October. The trunk had been shipped from Whitehorse and the airfreight charge was 54 cents a pound. In the days to come that trunk was an omnipresent reminder that I had commitments and my bride-to-be would soon be on her way to begin a new life together. In later years I would pretend that I had to go ahead with the wedding because I couldn't afford the airfreight costs to return the trunk.

CHAPTER NINE

Married on Top of the World

It carries me home to the one I hold dear
I'm there in her arms, she holds me so near
It's not all this snow or the cold that I fear
Only the wind that keeps blowing.

Only The Wind

WHILE I WAS STILL in Whitehorse Yukon, Iris and I decided that we would get married in Baker Lake. At the time it had seemed to be the most logical and convenient thing to do. She had to finish her tenure at the hospital and I had to take up my posting in Baker Lake without delay. Neither of us wanted a big wedding. 'A quiet ceremony without a lot of fuss,' was how we had described it. Little did we know at the time what a 'big deal' it would turn out to be. A major article about our wedding and honeymoon appeared in *The Canadian Magazine*, another in the *R.C.M.P. Quarterly* and several local magazines as well. All this was totally unplanned by us. I guess if a culprit were to be identified, it would have to be Iris' mother, and number one promoter. I think she even wrote a letter to Queen Elizabeth about the wedding. In any case, it was a letter written by Iris to her mother after our honeymoon that sparked all the interest.

Iris had arrived in Baker Lake in late October, and was staying with the Tanners until we were married. I had moved into the 'Game Cabin', as it was called, and was trying to make it habitable for my bride-to-be. Actually I wouldn't have blamed Iris if she had taken one look at the place and caught the next plane south. It was what one would call the 'open concept' in interior design. There were semi-partitions around the bed and the 'honey-bucket'. The top and bottom were left open to allow the warm air to circulate. In one corner sat a large galvanized water barrel. An oil-fired cook stove heated the building. It had one table and two chairs.

Gerry Tanner had gone out with me after midnight and we were able to requisition a double-bed and a fairly new washing machine from the government warehouse, so I thought we were making progress. So far Iris had taken everything in her stride and was busy with wedding preparations. I had already arranged with Alan Whitton, the Anglican minister, to perform the wedding in his church.

During the period prior to the wedding I had been busy organizing my first major project with the hunters and trappers. Caribou had been hard to find that fall and there wasn't much meat in town. I had discussed the idea of an organized community caribou hunt with my supervisor, Frank Bailey in Churchill. He gave me full support. The problem was we needed an aircraft to locate any caribou left in the country and aircraft in the Keewatin Region were difficult to charter at the best of times. Most companies were reluctant to send a small aircraft into the barren-lands in winter. The days went by without any word from Frank as to whether or not he had located an aircraft. Our wedding date was set for 16 November and by the 13th we still didn't have an aircraft to do any flying. I was ready to drop the idea, when on the 14th I received a radiogram from Frank. He would be arriving that day with a Cessna 180 on skis. I thought, 'What if we get out there and get weathered-in or something? Iris will kill me!' Her Mom and Dad and bridesmaid were flying in the same day from the south at considerable expense.

I let Iris know what was to happen and tried to make it sound routine. 'Just a couple of hours flying – no problem.'

The plane arrived with Frank, and plans were made to leave as soon as possible the next day. The hours of daylight were decreasing rapidly.

Just before noon on Friday the 15th we took off and headed northwest of Baker Lake. There was high cloud and visibility on the ground was marginal. I began to wonder if we would be able to see caribou if we flew right over them. Below the aircraft an endless sea of white slipped beneath us. The banks of the Thelon River provided a reference for a while until we turned west toward Schultz and Aberdeen Lakes. I was beginning to think the trip was a waste of time when suddenly we spotted a small band of caribou. Actually they showed up fairly well as they still had dark early winter coats. Later on they would appear almost white and would be almost impossible to spot from the air. We discovered several small herds in the area and I plotted the locations on my map. Three hours later we landed on the airstrip somewhat relieved that everything went so well and that we had been able to find caribou.

While I had been out flying, Iris' parents and bridesmaid, Karen Kalder, had arrived on Transair. I was 'conspicuous by my absence' as the saying goes and Iris' folks began inquiring as to my whereabouts. Gerry Tanner tried to reassure them.

'He's out doing some flying but he should be back any time now.'

'Well he better be back before tomorrow,' Iris' Dad commented. 'He better be here for the wedding!'

I had received an order from Sears the week before: a black suit and a pair of black shoes. I felt I was well prepared for the ceremony. John Ayageak, whom I had met because he had done some work for me, and David Mitchell, a young Bay clerk, had agreed to be best men. From my point of view anyway, it seemed things were ready. At 3:30 p.m. I dressed up, pulled on my parka and walked over to the church.

When I went inside the church I was really surprised because it was packed with people. More than one hundred crowded the pews. Most were Inuit, but I was pretty nervous by now and I really didn't notice who else was there. Hugh Ungungai had asked if he could play the organ for the service and I said I would be pleased if he would. He sat grinning at me from the organ bench.

John Tapatai sat beside him with his guitar. I was somewhat overwhelmed by the genuine interest everyone was taking in our 'quiet' wedding ceremony. Reverend Whitton gave a pleasant calming effect to the nervous minutes before the arrival of the bride. Soon I heard the throaty roar of the Bombardier snowmobile and I knew the waiting was over.

The bride entered the church on her father's arm resplendent in a wedding gown she had redesigned herself to better reflect a northern theme. It was a full length satin gown; white fur trimmed the neckline, sleeves and hem. She was radiant as she walked down the narrow aisle between the parkas and *amoutiks* of the congregation. At the pot-bellied stove situated in the middle of the church's only aisle, father and daughter separated. Iris had to skirt along one side of it and her father wedged carefully through on the other. Four-year-old Kelly Tanner, Gerry and Sheena's young daughter, was her flower girl.

The service was read, vows taken, rings exchanged, hymns sung, in Inuk-tit-tuut and English and all too soon we were signing on the line and climbing into the Bombardier.

A formal reception was held in the club house of the curling rink. Actually the building had been among one of the early wooden houses built by the Hudson's Bay Company and now donated to the community. It was decorated with wolf pelts and duffel tapestries made by local artists. The head table held a three-tiered wedding cake made and presented by Jean Kelly, wife of one of the Department of Transport employees. We received gifts from local people, including a beautiful soapstone carving of a ptarmigan by Frances Kalooar. We were quite amazed at the generosity and sincerity of the efforts made on our behalf. I tried, albeit ineffectively, to express our deep-felt appreciation.

The evening was a whirl of dancing, eating, and practical jokes. We were introduced to the Inuit square dance, a marathon of physical endurance. Everyone was having a great time. Iris and I served the wedding cake to the guests in the traditional manner. Reluctantly people began to pull on parkas and head out the door. At just the right moment Iris and I slipped out. We were sure our house was being watched so instead of going straight home I drove the Bombardier out to the airstrip to wait out the pranksters.

I parked the Bombardier and we visited and reviewed our memorable day. Little did we know just how memorable it was yet to become. 'They'll never guess where we are,' I commented. 'In an hour or so they'll get tired of watching for us to return to the cabin and go home.'

'I hope we don't have to sit out here that long,' Iris replied.

I switched off the motor to save gas. The inside began to cool off quickly so I hit the starter to warm up. To my astonishment I heard a faint 'click'. I hit the button again: 'Click, click.' The battery was dead.

'Oh no!' Iris lamented. 'What are we going to do?'

Humiliation made my face feel hot. We were stranded four kilometers from the village dressed only in light jackets. Iris was wearing a silky dress and it was minus 18°C outside!

'Well,' I said. 'There's no point sitting here so let's get walking before we get any colder.'

I took Iris' hand and we struck off down the road to the settlement. The darkness closed around us like a heavy cold curtain. In the distance the lights of the village beckoned us. We walked as fast as we could, occasionally running for short distances. There wasn't a chance anyone would be out on this road so late at night; we would have to make it on our own. Iris was freezing cold and almost exhausted. 'How could I do such a stupid thing?' I thought to myself. 'If anyone ever finds out about this I'll never live it down. Anyway, forget that for now, I've got to get Iris home.'

'It's just a bit further,' I said to encourage Iris. 'It wouldn't be right to freeze to death the first night of our marriage.' I put my arm around her waist to help her move faster. 'Not to mention the fact that we haven't even had a chance to consummate the whole deal,' I thought, and broke into a trot.

At long last we were on the fringe of the settlement. We struggled past the little church where only hours earlier we had pledged our love. By now we were both so cold we didn't care who we bumped into; we just wanted to get home. The streets remained empty as we scurried home. 'I don't think anyone noticed us,' I said as we entered the door.

I cranked the oil cook stove (our only source of heat) as high as it would go and watched as my new bride hovered within inches of the hot surface.

This made me nervous and I cautioned her not to stand so close. She spoke not a word as she turned from the stove and began to pull heavy long underwear over her stockings. I watched in amazement as she pulled another pair over the first. I began to doubt my chances of ever extricating her young body from those layers of material any time soon. With an unspoken finality she climbed shivering into bed and began pulling blankets over her head.

I stood by the stove warming myself and tried to think. What should my next move be? I cast a longing glance at the large hump in the middle of the bed and wondered if I should even try sleeping there. What a wedding night this was turning out to be.

My attention was diverted by the sound of voices outside the door. There was a crowd out there and they were trying to get in. I had had the forethought to wedge Iris' heavy trunk against the outside porch door and all the suitcases and heavy containers I could find. This proved useless as I noticed the door begin to bulge inward. I entered the porch and added my shoulder to the trunk. In the process I made some noise. I heard big Ed Henderson's voice boom, "Hey, they're in there!" What resulted next was the force of a bull moose hitting the door. The trunk and I shot backward and I watched in amazement as the door knob penetrated Iris' large suitcase. These people meant business so I conceded and yelled, 'Okay, take it easy, I'll let you in.'

There was much laughter and jostling as a dozen or more of our friends climbed in over the trunk and suitcases.

The next several hours were filled with much good-natured fun, most of it at our expense, but thankfully they did not know of our ordeal at the airstrip and they very kindly left my new bride under her pile of blankets undisturbed. I was required however to produce my guitar and serenade everyone with several songs. I tried to pick ones with appropriate lyrics such as 'So long it's been good to know you' and 'If only I could see my true love sleeping and if I could hear her heart softly pounding'. But to no avail. They all had a good laugh but no one got up to go. Finally they relented and prepared to leave. Ed Henderson, the six-foot-two RCMP constable, was quite apologetic about the damaged suitcase and porch door. 'Oh don't worry about it,' I laughed as I followed everyone to the door and bade them good-night. I crept quietly under the edge of the bed covering and lay staring up at the dark ceiling until I finally fell asleep.

I was jolted awake next morning around 8 a.m. by a loud knocking on the door. It was still dark out but as I peeped cautiously through the window I could make out Iris' father in the street light. 'What does he want?' I muttered.

He pounded on the door again and shouted, 'Time to go fishing!' It was then I remembered I had unwittingly promised to take him ice fishing the day before.

'Why did he have to get up so early?' I mumbled as I stumbled back to bed. I decided to ignore him. As I crawled back under the blankets I heard a faint voice from the other side of the bed.

'Who's pounding on the door?'

'It's your Dad ... he wants to go ice fishing.'

'Are you going to go?' The faint voice was a little stronger now.

'No,' I said. 'It's still night out there!'

The bedclothes rustled and I felt a warm body drawing close to me.

'I'm glad,' the voice replied.

Now there was a thumping on the wall.

'Just ignore it,' Iris said. 'One thing for sure, my Dad sure likes to fish.'

Finally the thumping stopped and we began to cuddle.

CHAPTER TEN

Honeymoon Caribou Hunt

I see the Northern Lights a'dancin high
Painting pretty pictures in the sky.

Mush Along

O N MONDAY MORNING, 18 November, I donned the caribou clothing that I had borrowed from the RCMP and my new bride dressed in the caribou skin *amoutik* that she had borrowed from Jean Ungungai, Hugh's wife, and we went down to the frozen surface of the lake where final preparation of the komatiks was taking place. Since the Game Management snowmobile was nothing but a ravaged shell, I had rented an 18 hp machine from one of the local residents. I hoped it was in good working order.

I was somewhat nervous about pulling the komatik on an eight-meter towrope, but that was the way it was done here and I was ready to give it a try. Iris' parents and Karen, her bridesmaid, had come down to the lake to see us off. I saw all the other hunters heading out across the lake and I didn't want to be left behind.

'Say good-bye to your folks and let's go!' I shouted back from the snowmobile. I pulled the starter cord and the engine barked to life. Iris barely had time for a few quick hugs and a hurried good-bye to her parents before she jumped on the top of the loaded komatik. I opened the throttle; the towrope tightened and the komatik lurched down the slope toward the lake ice. We were off. The rest of the party was already well out on the lake and I had to hurry to catch up. I looked back at Iris; she was hanging on with one hand and waving frantic farewells with the other. There were fifteen Inuit hunters, one RCMP Corporal, a Game Officer and his new wife in the group and I thought to myself as I steered the snowmobile over the uneven snowdrifts, 'This is going to be a day to remember.'

'I must be crazy,' I muttered. It was my first trip out on the land and here I was pulling my new wife along behind on a sled. I wasn't even sure I was going to be able to look after myself, let alone my bride.

Ellis and Iris on honeymoon caribou hunt.

At the confluence of the Thelon River and Baker Lake I followed the trail of the snowmobiles that were ahead of me as the leader picked his way through a jumble of ice blocks and rough snowdrifts. High winds during freeze-up had created this maze and I was about half way across when I passed the first casualty of the trip. An older model snowmobile had broken down and the owner had abandoned it. Apparently he had jumped on another sled, not willing to miss out on the hunt.

I glanced back at Iris hanging on tightly to the roped canvas cover as the long lumbering komatik lunged over each massive ice block. I was slowly getting the hang of towing the long sled and could quickly understand why the length of the sled and the towrope was very necessary. I was able to pick my way around obstacles with the snowmobile while the sled rode up and over, thumping down on the other side. A bit rough for the passengers, but otherwise making travel over rough terrain feasible.

When we reached the south side of the river and headed northwest, the going was much better. Soon I was sailing along at a nice clip and I turned and gave my bride a big wave. She returned it with a big smile, still grasping tightly to the ropes with the other hand.

I had the other hunters in sight by this time and we covered several miles without incident.

The land began to rise slightly and I noticed that the wind had blown some of the snow off the ridge we were now beginning to climb. The runners of the sleds were biting through to the gravel underneath. A glance ahead confirmed that we were getting into trouble. Some of the snowmobiles had spun out trying to move their heavy loads. Others were swinging clear, making their own trail beside the others, gunning the engines to maintain forward momentum. Once forward motion stopped you were stuck and it took a lot of work to get things moving again.

Despite my spinning track and howling engine, I was gradually losing speed. Soon I was down to a crawl. I turned back to Iris and yelled at the top of my voice, 'Get off and push!' Iris reminded me later that it was the first time in our marriage that I had yelled at her. She obediently jumped off the barely moving sled and began to run alongside pulling on one of the lashing ropes. Slowly we began to gain speed. I was avoiding the other snowmobile trails, blazing my own in the fresh snow. We began to gain more speed. By now Iris was merely running behind trying to catch up. I yelled again, 'Hurry; jump on, I can't stop!' She lunged forward, her legs thrashing beneath the bulky caribou skin *amoutik*. I slowed down as much as I dared. We passed several hunters who were stuck. With a final massive effort, Iris sprang forward and managed to grab the ropes that lashed the back of the load. Her legs dragged along behind until slowly she was able to pull herself forward, hand over hand, to the top of the load. I breathed a sigh of relief and opened the throttle. I glanced back at my passenger. No smiles or waves this time; she was hanging on with both hands glaring at me.

'Well,' I thought, 'all the other outfits have one or two men on their sleds to help if the going gets tough. Here I am, an inexperienced *Qallunaaq* and his slim little wife. Who's going to help me?'

The travel conditions were soon back to normal and we began to put miles behind us. I knew from my aircraft flight that we still had a long way to go.

Around noon I caught up with the leaders. They had stopped on a small lake for a 'mug-up'. It was a well-appreciated break. I went back to talk to Iris. I explained the consequences of stopping on the ridge and apologized for making her run so fast. She was so glad that I had finally agreed to take her on the trip that I knew if she had any misgivings she would keep them to herself.

'I'm alright,' she affirmed. 'It's a little rough; like riding a bucking horse but I'll be alright.'

After a quick cup of tea we pressed on. We were quickly running out of daylight. By three o'clock in the afternoon the sun had set and we traveled on in the twilight. We reached a fair sized lake and were about half way across when several outfits stopped. More bad news.

Scottie Tooloolee's big double track machine had broken down. Added to this was a broken ski on Hugh Ungungai's machine. This meant more doubling up. Since I was hauling 40 gallons of fuel plus other freight on my komatik and already had a heavy load to pull; the others took the passengers and their bedrolls. The rest was left behind with the machines.

On we traveled, now in total darkness. Little yellow pinpoints of light bouncing across a seemingly endless sea of white. I was amazed at the ability of the Inuit hunters to know where they were going. How were we to find a small rigid-frame cabin on the bleak shore of Schultz Lake in the darkness? I was in awe of their navigational skills. My admiration was slightly modified however when we drove on to a sand island with only a dusting of snow and all of the komatiks became stuck. Try pulling a 800 or 900 pound sled on sand. It makes for real tough sledding!

The only way to get moving again was to put nine or ten men on each komatik, pushing and pulling until we struck the good ice again. It was backbreaking work and it was very dark; the men around me chatting away in Inuk-tit-tuut were black moving forms whose features I could not recognize. Overhead the velvet sky was awash with trains of stars and in the northeast a modest display of the aurora lightened the horizon.

Soon, by working together, we managed to get all the outfits back on the ice. I talked to Iris and gave her a hug.

'It can't be much further,' I said. 'This is Schultz Lake and the cabin is on the north shore.'

'I hope we get there soon,' she answered in a tired voice.

By now everyone else had fired up their snowmobiles and were racing off across the lake. I started mine, but the wind had blown the ice free of snow in this area and I was unable to start my load. The snowmobile track just spun uselessly beneath me. I tried pulling it to one side but it was no use. I couldn't start the sled. Iris was by now standing alongside pulling as hard as she could. Still no results.

Finally I said. 'You come and drive this snowmobile and I'll push.'

I explained what was necessary to drive the snowmobile and we tried again without results. My caribou skin *kamiks* could not grip the glare ice and I was unable to apply much force to the komatik. By now everyone else had disappeared into the darkness.

'I guess we'll have to lighten the load!' I shouted to Iris and shut off the machine. I fumbled in the dark with the rope lashing and pulled off two drums of gas.

'We can pick it up on the way home,' I said, and then went forward and started the snowmobile.

'Now, you drive, Iris, and if I get the sled going don't slack off whatever you do or we'll be stuck again. We'll stop when we get on better footing.'

'Alright,' she said, 'but I've never driven one of these things before.'

'It's okay,' I yelled above the sound of the motor. 'Just keep the skis straight and push the throttle with your thumb.'

I grabbed the rope lashing and screamed. 'Okay. Now!'

The engine howled and the track beat a rhythm on the polished ice surface. Slowly I edged the komatik forward and the snowmobile began to move. We gathered a little speed and I started trotting alongside still pulling. Faster, faster, we were moving better now and I let go of the rope and ran for the back of the snowmobile. I was almost exhausted as I vaulted over the back of the snowmobile onto the seat. My arms went around Iris as I tried to keep my balance. She screamed and took her hands off the handlebars letting off the throttle. We began to slow to a stop.

'No! No!' I screamed. 'Don't let it stop!'

When she realized that I wasn't the imaginary polar bear she thought was leaping on her, she jammed her thumb down hard on the gas. By now we were back on the snow surface and the machine spurted ahead. The sudden acceleration snapped my head back and almost catapulted me backward off the snowmobile.

Eventually we got things under control and stopped on the hard-packed snow. When I had Iris safely seated on the komatik once again I wondered how I would find my way to a cabin I had never been to before. I glanced up to find the Big Dipper and Polaris. At least I knew the general direction we had to follow.

'I'll try to follow the trail left by the others,' I said reassuringly to my bride. 'I'm sure someone will come back if we don't show up.'

I ran across the tracks of another snowmobile and began to follow them with the headlight. We were engulfed in darkness but I traveled on following the faint tracks of the snowmobile. I estimated we had covered about 16 km when I finally caught up with the rest of the group. They were all sitting together on their komatiks waiting for me. I was much relieved to be back in the company of my hunter friends, who modestly possessed the necessary attributes that made it possible for them to travel and survive in this vast unforgiving country, even in total darkness.

It would take another hour or so of travel to bring us to the cabin. We arrived around 9:00 p.m. It had taken 13 hours to cover 137 km. Words are inadequate to describe the relief we felt to be safely at our destination.

The cabin, although small, looked very hospitable compared to the cold, windy night outside its walls. Some of the hunters began searching nearby for snow suitable for igloo building. They still had to build their houses before they would be able to eat and rest.

Hugh, Scottie, Ed, the RCMP Corporal, and two Inuit hunters shared the cabin with us. The newly-weds had the honor of sleeping on the small narrow bottom plywood bunk. It was not exactly what one would call a romantic honeymoon setting but we were so tired from the trip that it didn't really matter that much. The RCMP provided a security screen above us and four people slept on the floor beside us. Soon heavy breathing flooded the cabin but unfortunately it did not emanate from the lower bunk. I bade my new bride goodnight and fell asleep.

At first light, the area around the cabin bustled with activity as hunters prepared themselves for the impending hunt. Hugh joined us as we prepared the komatik for the day and we were glad for his cheerful presence.

Since I was not legally a resident of the NWT (which required six months residency) I could not hunt. I had no intention of setting a bad example to the Inuit people so I explained to Hugh that I wouldn't be shooting any caribou. He seemed disappointed, then brightened and said, 'Don't worry, there'll be plenty of meat.'

The group was ready and we departed along the north shore of the lake and then headed inland to the area where I had pinpointed the caribou on the map. A sobering thought flashed through my mind. 'What if I got the locations wrong? What if we couldn't find any caribou?' I barely had time to contemplate the embarrassment when we spotted caribou tracks in the snow. A lot of caribou tracks. Forward we sped with the lightly loaded komatik thumping along behind. As we topped a small rise, there in the distance were caribou; more than a dozen small groups of eight or nine animals.

From this point on, pandemonium reigned. Snowmobiles and hunters took off like a pack of wolves. Before long the shooting started and from that point my main concern was to stay out of the line of fire. The caribou scattered and the hunters did likewise in hot pursuit. Hugh sat down on the snow and started shooting at a small group of caribou passing in front of us. He managed to drop several before they ran out of range. The work of chasing down wounded animals and butchering began.

The next three days passed quickly. I kept busy collecting as much biological information as possible including the lower jaws for aging purposes. Everyone was in a good mood and were very cooperative while assisting me in taking measurements and collecting information. The hunters took a total of sixty-one caribou. This would bring much satisfaction to the families when they were hauled back to the settlement.

It was decided we would return to Baker Lake on Friday, 22 November.

Early in the morning we began to prepare for the return trip. All the extra caribou meat was cached inside the cabin. I would return later with the Bombardier snowmobile and haul it home.

As the sky lightened we headed off across the lake for home. We traveled as fast as conditions would permit in order to make the best use of the daylight hours. Finally we had to stop and refuel. Our outfit had been keeping up with the machines in the lead, putting the miles behind us. Hugh came over with Scottie who said something to me in Inuk-tit-tuut. Hugh interpreted for him. Scottie said, 'This *Tuktuluree* really likes to travel.' I took this as a compliment. Soon we were on the trail once again. Iris was getting tired from the fast pace, but she was as anxious as I was to get home. It was much colder now than on the trip out and the wind had hardened the drifts making travel at times difficult.

At our next stop Iris came up with a concerned look on her face. 'I have to go to the bathroom bad!'

It almost sounded comical. We were in the flattest part of nowhere and she wanted privacy.

'Well,' I said, as I finished fueling the skidoo, 'what do you want me to do?'

'Come with me,' she said somewhat irritated. 'Walk with me away from the others.'

We started walking. After 100 meters or so I stopped.

'Go further.'

'Why?' I asked. 'You could walk a mile and still not be out of sight.'

'Well, you stand in front of me then.'

I stood as she began to take off various layers of clothing. I noticed the group was getting ready to travel.

'Hurry up!' I said impatiently, 'They're starting to leave.'

'I am hurrying!' Iris screamed back angrily. 'I wish it was your backside freezing in the wind.'

I tried to help her with her clothing, but she wasn't in a good mood by this time.

'Just never mind!' she said. Finally we dashed to our outfit and started off after the rest.

'Men do have something of an advantage in this business,' I thought as we sped away.

The trip proceeded nicely until we were about 25 km from Baker Lake when everything began to fall apart. Hugh and Ed had been traveling with another outfit until the snowmobile broke down. They had to cache everything and find someone else to travel with. Since Iris was the only one on my sled, they decided to travel with me. By now everyone was scattered, some broken down, others ahead and behind, and now it was beginning to get dark.

We were following a small stream that we hadn't traveled on the outward journey. Owing to glare ice the traveling was treacherous. I was glad I had two men on the komatik to help control it. Often it would be headed toward big boulders frozen in the streambed and they would jump off and pull the sled out of harm's way. We were making very poor time. Just before we were to leave the stream the sled headed for some rocks. Hugh and Ed jumped off to change the direction of the outfit. One of them slipped on the glare ice and before they could gain control of the komatik it crashed into the rocks badly damaging the right runner.

I thought we should camp for the night and fix the komatik in the daylight. We were so close to home, this idea didn't sit well with any of us. Hugh thought we could cache our load of meat and supplies and fix the sled good enough to make it home. We decided to give it a try. On a komatik the runners are lashed to the cross-slats with strong cord. We pulled the runner that had collapsed as straight as we could and tightened the lashing. It still ran at a noticeable angle but we thought if we kept our weight over the good runner we could continue. We decided to try. Hugh said he knew a better route than the one we were following and since we were now in total darkness he drove the skidoo and I climbed on the sled with the others. It was like riding a balancing beam at about 20 kph. We started to get the hang of it and I began to think we might be able to make it home.

At about this moment a large pebble flew up from the towrope as we traversed a gravel area and struck me on the cheek. I almost lost my balance but managed to hang on. Iris checked my face; there was a little blood and she was concerned. I was glad I hadn't taken it in my eye. Hugh never looked back, just continued on at full speed. I said 'I'll be alright,' as we sped on in the darkness.

I was riding in the front and after several miles became very uncomfortable and tried to improve my seating a little. Big mistake; I lost my balance and fell off. The skidoo roared away into the night.

I lay in the snow looking up at the stars and almost laughed out loud. I knew I wasn't hurt from the fall off the sled and I thought what a circus this whole trip had become. I determined that in the future, things would be different. Perhaps a better back-up contingency or something.

I got up eventually and began to walk along the skidoo trail which I could still faintly see in the starlight. When I couldn't see it any longer I would lie down on the snow and wait for daylight. It would be foolhardy to walk around in the dark. I was wearing my caribou clothing and knew I wouldn't freeze. I really didn't expect Hugh to look back to see if he still had a komatik until he got to the settlement. I should have insisted that we make camp back there on the little river.

I walked along for a while and before long I could see the yellow bouncing light of a snowmobile coming back along the trail.

'Well, what do you know,' I muttered to myself. 'I wonder what made him turn his head.' I learned later from Iris that they had bounced into a ridge of gravel with very little snow and the skidoo spun out. I jumped on behind Hugh and we drove back several kilometers to where the others waited. Iris was really anxious thinking I might have been injured.

We hauled the sled out of the gravel and hitched up. Before we started again I called Hugh to one side and stated firmly, 'Look Hugh, I want you to slow this machine down, we're not running a race here, and turn your damn head once in a while! We're trying to stay on this broken sled but it's not easy.'

Hugh could see I was pretty mad and he gave assurances that things would be better. We climbed aboard and pushed on.

At the mouth of the Thelon, with the lights of the settlement in the distance, we came across an abandoned komatik. It was in good order and we quickly transferred our load and headed for the welcome lights of home.

The Game Cabin looked like a palace as we walked toward it. It was freezing inside as someone had turned down the stove to conserve oil and we had to keep our parkas on until it warmed up. We were mighty glad to be home. My cheek that had taken the stone was swollen badly but we considered ourselves lucky. I had learned a lot about traveling on the tundra in winter and was sure future trips would be better.

On 24 November I headed back on our trail with the Bombardier snowmobile to pick up our cached meat, broken sleds and other gear. I met several snowmobiles on their way home. Owing to bad weather it was 6 December before I made it back to the cabin on Schultz Lake to haul in the rest of the caribou meat. Everyone in the village was pleased to receive a good supply of meat before Christmas.

Despite all the difficulties I will always consider it a worthwhile project, a great adventure and certainly a honeymoon to remember.

CHAPTER ELEVEN

Trip to Parker Lake

So I'm cutting blocks of snow
And in my igloo I will go.

Mush Along

SINCE MY ARRIVAL in September, I was preoccupied with getting the twelve-passenger Bombardier snowmobile repaired and reliable enough to use for extended trips on the land. It had been a frustrating experience. I was barely on speaking terms with the Government's head mechanic. The Bombardier was in poor condition following a disastrous trip Hugh had taken the previous winter. It needed a lot of fixing and I just couldn't seem to get the mechanic to work on it. Things took a turn for the better when the mechanic was replaced.

Roy Emery, the new mechanic, was like a breath of fresh air. He practiced his trade with a high degree of efficiency. It seemed he could fix just about anything and even build something new if necessary.

On 17 December 1969, Roy and I tested the Bombardier snowmobile after extensive repairs had been completed. After a short trip to Prince River it was pronounced in good running order. I made plans to leave the next morning for Parker Lake.

On Hugh's infamous trip of the previous winter he had left Game Management equipment abandoned along his route. The purpose of my trip was to see if I could retrieve some of it. The main item was a large covered sled that had been built to pull behind the Bombardier. I needed such a sled badly so this was the main purpose of the trip.

We left Baker Lake around 7 a.m.; hours before daylight. The first part of the trip was across Baker Lake and all that was required was to maintain the right direction until the sun came up. Hugh, Scottie Tooloolee, Jacob Ickeeneelee and Matthew Koonungnat had asked to go along. Jacob knew that part of the country well as did Scottie, so I was pleased to have them along.

The trip was somewhat monotonous as we motored along at about

Hugh Ungungai with Skidoo snowmobile.

20 kph. The southeastern sky began to redden around 10:30 a.m. and soon the sun struggled above the horizon a few degrees and hung there. It looked like a partially squashed tomato casting weak rays through a halo of cloud and ice crystals.

Just before we left the south shore of Baker Lake we crossed a small pressure ridge. It was only a meter high and we had little trouble finding a safe place to cross. Traveling overland one had to be alert for large snow covered rocks, which, if struck, could cause damage to the skis or front suspension of the Bombardier.

The wind picked up slightly as we reached the surface of Bissette Lake and soon we were traveling in a moderate ground drift. Everything was white, but I slowed down and tried to maintain a straight line across the lake. I failed completely. Scottie, who was deaf but could read lips in Inuk-tit-tuut suddenly started gesturing and calling for me to stop. I thought he wanted to get out to relieve himself, so I stopped. We all got out and there was much chatter which, of course, I could not understand. Scottie was walking back and forth, peering into the snowy haze. After a minute or two I asked Hugh if there was a problem. He looked concerned as he spoke, 'They think we're going in the wrong direction.' The Inuit were checking the wind and the direction of the snow ridges. I realized that we were now driving into the wind. This couldn't be right. You don't get a south wind up here in December. We should be traveling downwind. Crossing the lake I had somehow slowly turned in a wide arc until I was headed back almost the way I had come. I could hardly believe it possible, but there was now no doubt. Old Scottie had sensed it and called for a halt.

'Man, this country is scary at times,' I mumbled to Hugh as we got back in and turned the machine around. I threw open the roof hatch and my companions took turns navigating across the lake.

Several hours passed as we continued to roll south and east. The sun set around 2:30 p.m. and we went on in the twilight. I had hoped we could make it to where the sled was abandoned but as the light began to fail I wondered if this would be possible.

Another halt was called and Jacob climbed up on a rocky knoll for a look around. There was much discussion when everyone gathered again beside the snowmobile. Hugh said, 'We're close. Not too sure exactly where we are but it shouldn't be too far to the lake.' We piled in and drove a few more kilometers. More stops, more looking around, then on again. The sky cleared and the twilight held a little longer. Finally Jacob affirmed that he knew where we were and gave me the direction with a sweep of his arm. Off we went again and soon I saw a dark object against the whiteness. 'That's the komatik,' Hugh announced and in minutes we drove alongside.

I backed the Bombardier to where I could hitch a chain on the big sled and promptly got the machine stuck in soft deep snow that had accumulated around this obstacle to the ever-present north wind. I was tired and frustrated. I began the tedious task of digging the snow out from between the tracks of the machine where it was high-centered. I used a large 'jack-all' to lift the back end a little to make the job easier.

I left the jack and started digging. What followed was almost a tragic accident. Old Scottie, who was taking intense interest in the proceedings, came along and for some reason put his hands on the handle of the jack-all. The slight downward pressure caused the handle to fly up and since he was not holding it firmly it shot through his hands and caught him under the chin. Down he went, as if he had been 'pole-axed'. I ran quickly to him as he lay on the snow unconscious. He was still breathing and soon he started to moan. Seconds later he began to spout a string of Inuk-tit-tuut phrases which I could not understand. I imagined he was cursing the *Qallunaaq* and all his weird dangerous contraptions. Using Hugh as an interpreter I was able to determine that he was not seriously hurt.

By 6 p.m. I finally had the Bombardier out of the deep snow. My companions had been building an igloo and soon we had a Coleman stove going and ice melting for tea. After a good supper we sat around telling stories in the soft glow of candlelight. Good-natured Hugh acted as interpreter as we spent an enjoyable time in the igloo visiting. Soon we began to gather our caribou skins and sleeping robes to bed down for the night.

The next morning I awoke in the pale light of the igloo's dome. The sun would not rise for hours but the bright stars overhead and a dancing aurora illuminated the faint outline of the snow-blocks so expertly cut and placed to form this comfortable haven in an otherwise hostile environment.

A candle was lit and soon the hissing and sputtering of the Coleman stove indicated that tea was being brewed.

I reflected momentarily on the events that had brought me to this place. The people I had met. The beautiful land that I had been privileged to view in pristine splendor. I was glad to be here with Inuit friends who seemed so much at ease in these austere surroundings.

The return trip went fairly well. The weather was marginal due to the incessant north wind and ground-drift but I was able to follow our old tracks and this made travel easier. The headlights picked up the tracks clearly but as the brief daylight period arrived near whiteout conditions developed and I repeatedly drove off the trail. I began wishing for darkness again so we could continue home on the same route we had followed the previous day.

Darkness did arrive around 2:30 in the afternoon and we continued to put miles of tundra behind us. Before long we were back on the ice of Baker Lake. I anticipated that the big plywood covered sled I was towing would give us endless trouble, but on the contrary, owing to a light load of equipment inside it trailed along nicely in the tracks made by the Bombardier.

I was following our old trail when suddenly the tracks seemed to rise up into the air and disappear into the black dome above the headlight beams. I slammed on the brakes. Hugh who had been dozing in the front passenger's seat, jerked awake. 'What happened?' he mumbled.

'I don't know,' I said. 'But something sure looks weird.'

By now all my passengers were alert and staring through the front windshield. Their discourse in their native tongue flowed fluently.

I got out and walked forward in the headlight beams. In several minutes I was able to understand what had happened. The old Bombardier tracks did indeed tilt upwards, ending abruptly at the edge of a huge slab of ice. We were at the pressure ridge we had crossed so easily the previous day. Now it had pushed up with the tremendous force of expanding ice into a jumbled mess, which was now over six meters high.

Hugh came up beside me and I said, 'How do we get over that?'

The others gathered around. There was much discussion and finally Hugh summed things up.

'We'll have to go along the edge and try to find a better place to cross.' We turned back to the idling Bombardier.

'I wonder how far we will have to go?' I said to no one in particular as I slipped the snowmobile into low gear.

We skirted the edge of the now huge pressure ridge and I marveled at the force of nature that was being played out here. I had a lot to learn about pressure ridges and in later years they would be the source of much trouble in my Arctic travels.

We drove seven or eight km along the ice ridge before we found a break. Cautiously we checked it over before attempting to cross it. We came over intact and this proved to be the last hurdle we would face. Across the frozen whiteness of the lake the welcome lights of the settlement twinkled like earth-bound stars as the Chrysler Industrial engine purred contentedly, driving us ever closer to home.

CHAPTER TWELVE

Flirting with the Grim Reaper

We'll die in the Arctic, and no one will know
Only the wind that keeps blowing ...

Only The Wind

THERE WAS A LOT OF SICKNESS in Baker Lake during the fall and early winter of 1968. I had a cold as a constant companion all through November. I thought I had finally shaken it off, but some trips out on the land and a lot of cold nights sleeping in igloos kept the cold bug circulating.

Our first Christmas together was memorable. We decorated a little green plastic Yum-Yum tree Iris had received from Regals and lit a few bright candles. We went out caroling despite the -45°C temperatures.

It was a big night of celebrating on New Year's Eve that finally gave me a real wake-up call. We had guests over for New Year's Day dinner and I couldn't wait for them to leave. My head felt like someone was pounding it with a sledge-hammer. Finally we were alone.

'You're burning up!' Iris announced as she felt my forehead.

'I'm not surprised,' I replied as I headed off to find the aspirins and go to bed.

The next 24 hours were like a weird nightmare as I drifted in and out of delirium. Iris had consulted with nurse friends and they had advised her to 'get him out on the next plane'. The new nurse at the nursing station had just arrived and wasn't too helpful. She obviously didn't like the place and couldn't wait to get back down south.

I was in a bit of a stupor on Friday, 3 January as Iris helped me get ready to go to the plane. Gerry Tanner had thoughtfully arranged to pick me up just before the plane was ready to depart so I wouldn't have to wait around in the cold. I vaguely remember him driving me to the plane in the Bombardier and helping me on the plane and into a seat. It was the cold DC3 and I was sitting near the back. The flight was like a bad dream. I remember looking off to the west after we had taken off and seeing the orange glow of the afternoon sun sitting on the horizon. Shortly it was dark and even in my warm goosedown clothing I was cold.

It seemed like eternity before we reached Churchill. Frank Bailey was there to meet me, and assist me off the plane.

'You don't look very good,' he said as he helped me into a government vehicle and drove me to the hospital. I was too sick to speak.

Without Frank I might never have been admitted. He answered all the questions he could for me. I remember waking up on the examining table and there were two people with me: a nurse, and a man whom I assumed was a doctor. I remember asking if I could move.

'Don't you dare!' the nurse exclaimed loudly. They were just preparing to insert a needle into my spine.

When I woke up again an orderly was wheeling me down a hallway. Having an intense fear of operating rooms from a childhood tonsillectomy I called out hysterically, 'Where are you taking me?'

'To the ward,' the man said and I slipped back into oblivion.

The next 24 hours were blurred. I remember vomiting and nurses assisting me. The rest was blackness. When I finally started to come around I learned I had meningitis and was in isolation.

It took two weeks in the hospital before I began to feel better. I temporarily lost my hearing and some of my sight. I was sitting on my bed one afternoon trying to write. I couldn't seem to get my hand and brain working together. I looked up and Iris was standing there. It was so good to see her again. She stayed in Churchill during the last week in hospital and visited me every day.

The doctor didn't like the idea of me going back up north. He said I should take at least a month to recuperate. I promised to take things easy and so I was discharged.

Iris and I took residence in a tiny hotel room right above the bar-room in the Hudson Hotel. It was the only room available. It was our great misfortune that the hotel had engaged an erotic dancer from down south who began her performance precisely at 11:30 p.m. every evening. She danced to a Buck Owen's record. I couldn't even imagine how she could keep anyone interested with a Buck Owen's tune, but I guess she managed. The performance usually lasted until midnight. We didn't even think of sleeping until the music was finished. Every night it was the same. We were in that little hotel room for five days before we were able to get on a plane for Baker Lake.

CHAPTER THIRTEEN

To Chesterfield Inlet by Boat

Eons of time, breaking my mind
When I see all these wonders
Sculptured by eons of time.

Eons of Time

D URING THE FIRST WEEK of September 1969, I decided that it was time to make contact with the people of Chesterfield Inlet. Perhaps I could encourage them with their trapping effort and make them aware of the Government's Fur Marketing program. My main problem was how to get there. There were no scheduled flights to this community 288 km (as the seagull flies) east of Baker Lake on the west coast of Hudson Bay.

I knew Thomas Tapatie owned a Peterhead boat. He was getting on in years and rarely made any trips with it. It was a common sight to see it riding at anchor just offshore from the Anglican Mission. I asked Hugh to inquire if Thomas would consider chartering the craft for a trip to Chesterfield Inlet. Word came back that he would make the trip and a fee was negotiated and a departure date set.

When Iris heard of the proposed trip she begged me to let her go along. I was very reluctant because I wasn't sure of what to expect on such a trip. We could strike a lot of stormy weather at this time of year. 'Why would you want to go?' I moaned. 'You're eight months pregnant!'

Iris began to articulate all the reasons why she should come. Her strongest argument was the fact that this would be the last chance to travel before she was tied down raising children. This was a big boat and hadn't I reassured her of how safe it would be even in stormy seas? It soon began to sound like it would be impossible to make the trip without her so despite my many misgivings, I agreed to let her come. I had to admit she hadn't been on many trips since the honeymoon caribou hunt. Maybe it wouldn't be too bad.

The weather was good on the morning of our departure and held for the whole day. The trip down the lake was slow and just a bit monotonous.

The lake is 100 km long with only a few large islands, so there really wasn't much to see. By late afternoon we had reached Christopher Island near the eastern end of the lake. As the sun dipped behind a scattered overcast sky on the western horizon we entered the north channel of Chesterfield Inlet. We took several photographs of the steep rocky shores, the ripple behind the boat reflecting the setting sun, but nothing was able to capture the true beauty of that fleeting scene.

We entered Cross Bay as the light began to fail and anchored for the night. Iris and I would pitch a tent on shore, the rest would sleep on board. Hugh came with us in the canoe so he could return with it to the Peterhead, thus saving the work of hauling it above the high tide mark. After he dropped us off, I pitched the tent and lit the Coleman stove for tea. The water was salty here but it wasn't difficult to find a fresh water stream nearby. Soon we were comfortably settled for the night. Iris and I had both enjoyed the rugged beauty of the North Channel and she expressed how very glad she was to be on the trip. I too was glad she was with me and I became less apprehensive as the trip progressed.

We were awake before daybreak and before long had the preparations for breakfast underway. The sky was brightening in the east as we packed up our gear and took down the tent. Matthew Koonungnat paddled the canoe over from the Peterhead and picked us up. Thomas started the Wisconsin air-cooled engine that powered the boat and we were soon underway.

We traveled between steep rocky cliffs that rose up sharply from the water. Flocks of Canada geese took flight ahead of us. High above the cliffs now crimson in the morning sun, a peregrine falcon flew an irregular course above the ridge searching for prey.

As we followed the north shore of Cross Bay, Hugh and Matthew took off in the canoe to hunt seals. Before long they were back with a plump ring seal in the bottom of the canoe. Hugh said they had shot another but it sank before they could retrieve it.

We were just leaving Cross Bay following the ever-widening channel of Chesterfield Inlet, when someone spotted a beluga whale surfacing ahead. The boat hummed with excitement and anticipation. If they could kill a beluga, that would make the trip very worthwhile to the hunters. Hugh and Matthew were off again in the canoe and Thomas diverted the Peterhead from his course in the direction of the whale sighting.

The whale surfaced several more times but only momentarily and not long enough for a shot. A harpoon was prepared and while Thomas navigated, I took a position on the bow with the harpoon. The whale did not make another appearance and after scanning the waters carefully we finally gave up the chase. Iris enjoyed the excitement regardless of whether or not we were successful. I think she was cheering for the whale.

As we cruised pleasantly along, Hugh, who liked to visit, told me that the Hudson's Bay Company supply ship had been late coming not too many years ago and as it was trying to reach Hudson Bay before freeze up got caught in a cold snap and froze in for the winter in Cross Bay. The captain was pretty angry because he had to evacuate the crew back to Baker Lake. He went on to say that the ships coming in to Baker Lake now always use the South Channel to get through to the lake because the channel is a little wider and deeper.

'Why didn't we use the South Channel?' I inquired.

'You have to catch the tide just right otherwise you can get caught in a big whirlpool and slammed into the rocks.' He paused for a few seconds then went on. 'There's a story about a hunter in a kayak who got sucked into that whirlpool years ago. The old people still talk about it. He disappeared and the other hunters thought he had drowned but he came back to the surface further down and was okay.'

I found Hugh's stories fascinating and as I recalled how our eight meter long Peterhead was gripped by the tidal currents in the North Channel and pushed about despite the power of the engine, I was glad we had taken the safer route. The old man used neither chart nor tide tables, but I felt confident with his many years of experience and the calm assured way in which he handled the boat. 'It would be nice to see that whirlpool someday,' I thought.

As the morning progressed we reached Primrose Island and by early afternoon we were churning into the widening channel at Barbour Bay. The scenery continued in rugged beauty. Many small streams came down to the irregular shoreline and we passed several rocky islands.

The lack of lavatory facilities on the boat presented a problem which Iris obviously had considered carefully. Perhaps memories of the honeymoon trip still lingered. Rather than delaying the boat and going ashore, she had decided to use a plastic garbage bag in the small forward cabin should it become necessary.

On the long stretch across Barbour Bay Iris caught my arm. 'You watch the hatch, I'm going to the bathroom in the cabin.' I closed the hatch behind her and stood guard.

Soon she re-surfaced and discreetly slipped the black plastic bag overboard. Suddenly there was excitement near the back of the boat as Hugh and Matthew scrambled for their rifles.

'*Nassiq! Nassiq!*' they shouted as they aimed at the black 'seal' which had suddenly surfaced in the boat's wake. When everyone finally realized it was a plastic bag I was already killing myself laughing. Iris' face glowed like the setting sun.

By late afternoon we could see the Wag and Promise Islands which marked the end of the Inlet and the beginning of Hudson Bay. On we sailed and soon we could see the radio mast which marked the settlement of Chesterfield Inlet.

It was necessary for us to continue past this sentinel as we had to round the long peninsula before we could sail up into the bay on which the settlement was situated. Around 7 p.m. we dropped anchor just offshore of the Hudson's Bay Company Post. Everyone was up-beat. Iris smiled as she announced cheerfully 'We made it!' My mind was already on the return journey and I was secretly hoping that there would be some way to get Iris back home other than by boat. I would have to look into the possibilities. For now we would set up our tent and get on with the work I had come here to accomplish.

The Inuit hunters and trappers of Chesterfield Inlet were friendly and willingly called a meeting for me. I explained why I had come: to see if there were ways in which I could assist them in getting more from the natural resources of the area. Most of the speakers were cooperative but really couldn't see how they could make a living from the land any more. They, like many others, I judged, had succumbed to the subtle but unrelenting pressures of the Government and other agencies to become townspeople. '*Tuktuluree*, you show me how I can make money on the land' was one statement made quite emphatically from one Inuk. I had invited Thomas Kakimut on the trip because he was one of the best white fox trappers in Baker Lake. Thomas addressed the meeting explaining his trapping efforts and the prices he had been receiving through the Fur Marketing Program.

I explained the assistance that they could get through the Fur Marketing Program of the Territorial Government which would give them another option other than simply taking the Bay price for their furs. Three or four hunters expressed a real intent to try white fox trapping again. But of course there was a problem why it couldn't be done. There were no August caribou skins in the settlement. Without caribou clothing it would be impossible to live and travel on the land.

I didn't ask why they hadn't hunted for clothing skins (August-killed skins are the only ones suitable for making clothing). I remembered the 200 plus skins I had bought from the hunters north of Yellowknife and took a chance.

Hugh was acting as interpreter so I said. 'What if I could get you some August caribou skins, would you go out trapping?'

Everyone assured me that they would.

I remember well the follow-up. I did ship them the skins a month later (most were destined for Coral Harbour since there were no caribou on Southampton Island). The query came back to me a week later. 'We got the skins and we'd like to know who's going to make the clothing.' I threw up my hands in exasperation.

Later that same afternoon after the meeting had dispersed, I was heading back to our tent when I heard an aircraft. I was surprised to see a twin-engine Grumman Goose amphibian aircraft circling the settlement. The plane landed in the bay and a canoe headed out to pick up the crew.

I knew the plane belonged to Pooch Lisenfeld of Rainy Lake Airways. He owned the Baker Lake Tourist Lodge and flew fishermen from the south up to Chantry Inlet for Arctic char.

'I'll bet he's on his way to Baker right now,' I said to Iris as we stood in front of our tent on the sandy shoal. 'You know, Iris, I'd feel a lot better if you went back on the plane; if I can get you a ride.' She must have read concern on my face, for she replied quietly. 'If you will feel better about things, I'll go.'

'Yes, I think I would,' I said. 'The weather has been good but it can change so fast and it is a worry.'

'If you can get me on that plane, I'll go,' she said without reservation.

I found out that Pooch was heading to Baker Lake but not until the next day. He had lots of room as there were only three passengers traveling with him. When I offered to pay the fare he refused.

'I'm going anyway,' he said as he dismissed the matter with a wave of his hand.

We intended to leave in the Peterhead at first light the next morning so I arranged for Iris to stay in the Mission overnight. We spent the rest of the afternoon walking around the settlement. We toured the old RCMP post and went to see the Mission's greenhouse. Green lettuce flourished in the small glassed building. It had been some time since either of us had viewed this delicacy. Our next stop was the chicken house. Hugh had informed us that they had a flock of chickens and might have eggs to sell. Sure enough, we were able to purchase three dozen and that night for supper we dined sumptuously on fresh eggs.

Before darkness fell I walked Iris over to the Mission complex where she would stay. Saying good-bye was extremely difficult. I hugged her tightly and held my hand on her protruding belly. 'Take good care of yourself and our little one,' I whispered.

'And you take care too and have a safe trip home.' With tears in our eyes we parted and I headed back to our tent.

The wind had risen and the sail-silk tent flapped and rustled as the swell off the bay crashed on the sandy shoal, making sleep difficult. I tossed fitfully for hours before finally sliding into a light slumber. When dawn broke I was making tea and packing my bed roll.

We weighed anchor as soon as we could see clearly and headed around the point into the teeth of a northerly gale. The Peterhead rode the increasing swells gracefully but a decided mist from the bow cutting the next swell sent a cloud of spray amid-ship. The motor did not have a protective cover. I donned my long rain slicker and held one side of a piece of tarp to keep the spray off the engine. I knew that once we sailed around the peninsula and into the inlet, things would improve. This took longer than anticipated as Thomas, who now held the wheel, reduced our forward speed to lessen the force of the on-coming combers. After some time we began to feel the protection of Rockhouse Island as we skirted its southern shore. The tarp was no longer needed, and Matthew and I took a well-earned rest.

Hugh hadn't shown himself and was presumably sleeping in the small forward cabin. I slid the hatch open and looked in. There was Hugh, still in a deep sleep. The forward deck was leaking due to the heavy swells and an intermittent stream of ice-cold water was falling down on Hugh's neck. He moaned and moved his head to one side but did not awaken. The top of his sleeping robe was soaking-wet and yet he slept oblivious to all. I could hardly keep from laughing. If that had been me I would have been up like a shot at the first drip. Not Hugh. 'It must be something pathological,' I muttered to myself as I slid the hatch shut.

As we sailed northwest up the Inlet, I kept my eyes glued to the southern horizon. Pooch had said they would probably leave around 10 a.m. and I hoped to catch sight of the plane as it sped westward. My vigilance was rewarded for just as we were reaching the wide stretch at Barbour Bay I caught sight of the Grumman Goose flying along the south shore. I was elated and relieved. 'She'll be home in a little over an hour,' I calculated and then set about firing up the Coleman stove to brew some tea.

We made Cross Bay before darkness overtook us and dropped anchor in the shelter of two islands. I slept on the boat. When dawn broke we churned back through the North Channel catching the high tide, which made the water as placid as a mill pond.

There was a distinct feeling of fall in the air as I sat sunning myself on the forward deck. The sun was bright but the air was crisp. Baker Lake stretched to the horizon before us. I was anxious to get home and this made the trip down the lake seem endless. As the western sky began to slowly lose the intensity of a crimson sunset, we passed Prince River and could discern the village on the northwestern shore.

CHAPTER FOURTEEN

A Son is Born

Listen to the tales that the wind will sing,
Stories of sadness and longing.

Only The Wind

IN THE NORTHWEST TERRITORIES women in their first pregnancy were required to leave remote villages at least six weeks before their due date. If they didn't, the airline could refuse to let them on their aircraft. The expectant mothers were advised to go to the nearest place where complete medical services were available. For people in Baker Lake, this was Churchill, Manitoba. This created real hardship for almost all those who had to follow this procedure but there was little anyone could do to improve the system.

We had decided well in advance that Iris would fly back to Saskatchewan rather than pining away in Churchill. Since she didn't want to have her child in her home town, we had arranged for her to stay with my older brother, his wife and family in Prince Albert. Eva, his wife, had given birth to seven children, so I thought she might have a few tips to pass along to Iris. The first good advice we received was the recommendation of a very good obstetrician.

It was a sad and emotional time on 19 November 1969 as she prepared to leave home. Everything was packed and ready well before plane time. We decided to go for one last walk together. We wandered slowly down to the lake and walked out on the frozen surface. It was a calm afternoon. Snowmobiles whined up and down the lake as the riders enjoyed the afternoon. We didn't talk much; just held hands as we walked along glancing occasionally at one another. We knew the next few weeks would be a trying time for both of us. We stopped for some pictures beside the caboose I had just finished building for use behind the Bombardier, then wandered home to get Iris' things.

The planes were still landing at the gravel airstrip as the ice strip on the lake in front of the settlement was not finished, so I drove Iris out in the Bombardier. The last few moments were difficult as I helped her up the steps into the aircraft.

'I'll be out for Christmas,' I told her as I let go of her hand. 'You can count on it.'

'I know,' she replied. 'The time will go quickly, you'll see.'

I watched the Transair DC3 until it was a small black dot in the southern sky before I headed back to the loneliness that I sensed awaited me.

Frank Bailey, my boss in Churchill, sent me a radiogram in early December advising me that he would be in Baker Lake on the 16th of the month with a Lambair single-engine Otter. He was planning a trip to Coral Harbour on Southampton Island and then south to Coats Island where several families from the settlement were spending the winter. He said if there was any work that needed an aircraft, he would make the Otter available.

I had attempted a trip to take fuel oil to Scottie Tooloolee's camp at the narrows south of Parker Lake with the Bombardier but the machine had started giving me trouble and I had to cache the fuel and return to Baker Lake for repairs. The old man was pretty upset. He was wintering in the camp in the surplus 'cracker box' house I had hauled down the previous spring. He wanted oil for his stove badly. I planned to drop off two 45 gallon drums with the Otter before we headed to Coral Harbour.

Frank arrived in the Otter just ahead of a three day blizzard. The wind got so bad that we couldn't even get down to the lake to check the condition of the aircraft. Don Boone was the pilot and he had a helper with him. He had flown in the Arctic for a while and knew how to tie down an aircraft. He didn't seem too worried about the storm.

I would fly with Don on several occasions after this trip and I felt he was a competent pilot. He would unfortunately lose his life in later years when a load of steel shifted in a Bristol Freighter he was piloting to Rankin Inlet. The Bristol crashed on the sea ice.

'If it's not tied down good enough, there's nothing we can do about it now anyway,' Don offered cheerfully as we watched the snow climb higher up the picture window of my new house. The wind howled like a banshee without let-up for three days and nights. On 19 December, we were able to get to the aircraft and confirm that it had survived intact. By 10 a.m. the following day we were loaded, warmed up and ready to leave. The wind still blew but visibility was much improved. We couldn't wait much longer if we were to get the mail and supplies to the people on Coats Island before Christmas.

I looked the single-engine Otter over carefully as we were loading it. It was still in the color and stripes of the Swedish Air Force. Lambair had just acquired it and immediately pressed it into service.

'I hope the engine is in good shape,' I thought as I climbed in. I knew we would be flying over open sea on the trip to Coats. The mere thought of it sent my heart-rate up a notch or two.

As we lifted off the ice strip and continued in over the settlement, I gazed down at our house with huge drifts from the recent storm hugging three sides. I wondered when Iris and I would live there again, together as a family. We turned and flew southeast across the frozen expanse of the lake. In the distance I could distinguish the flat truncated top of Sugar Loaf Mountain. The wind was somewhat stronger further south and the ground-drift made it difficult to distinguish land from ice. After circling the south end of Parker Lake, we were ready to give up when we finally managed to spot the square, black outline of Scottie's cabin. Now the challenge was to find a safe place to land nearby. The pilot circled before making a dry run over the area. We began our final descent. I looked forward through the windscreen and could see an area of rough, heavy snowdrifts where I reckoned we would touch down. Not to worry, I was sure the pilot would apply power to carry us over. Power was applied but the engine coughed and sputtered before it finally caught.

'Did you forget your carb heat, Don?' I thought, then bang! … we hit the rock-hard drifts. The oil drums shot forward against their restraining ropes. Frank sitting across from me uttered an oath. We were airborne again momentarily then landed hard again. This time Don kept the skis on the snow as we bounced across the drifted ice surface.

We coasted to a stop and turned around. Don kept the engine idling. Frank, still muttering, unstrapped himself and followed me to the back of the aircraft.

'He nearly killed us!' Frank gasped as we opened the back door.

'Yah; that wasn't one of his better landings, that's for sure. He didn't get the power on when he needed it.'

I began to unlash the oil drums. When I looked out I saw a diminutive figure approaching the plane through the hazy ground-drift. As he ran I recognized Barney Sitowak, a young hunter who was staying with old Scottie at his camp.

'Where's the old man?' I shouted over the idling engine.

'He's gone hunting,' Barney replied. He pressed some letters into my hand. 'Please take these to Baker.'

'I'll get them there,' I said then added, 'We have some grub and fuel oil for the camp.'

By now Don's assistant was rolling the drums back to the door. We shoved everything off and rolled the drums out of the way. I waved good-bye to Barney and climbed back aboard.

Don taxied to the smoothest area he could find, turned into the wind and pushed the throttle to the fire-wall. The Otter roared, bounced, hopped, touched, then one more bounce and we were airborne into the stiff, ever-persistent north-wind.

We flew northeast to Chesterfield Inlet where we landed and fueled the aircraft. I glanced at my watch: 1:20 p.m.; we would be in Coral Harbour just before dark.

The Otter thundered out over Hudson Bay. I listened carefully to the throb of the engine for any hint of trouble. It sounded just like all single Otters: as if the motor was going to fly apart at the next stroke. I tried to relax but the black water and floating ice pans below made this difficult. I was glad when Cape Kendall showed up dead ahead and we began flying over Southampton Island.

The Department of Transport fuel man was waiting for us at the airstrip. Lorne Stevenson the Settlement Manager arrived a few minutes later with a Bombardier to take Frank and me to the village. The pilot and his 'side-kick' would be staying at the DOT facility.

'Sure not much daylight these days,' someone remarked.

The man who fueled the plane replied, 'Oh well, it's going to be a whole lot better tomorrow.'

It was the winter solstice; tomorrow would be 22 December.

I occupied the rest of the afternoon and evening in the settlement office bringing the fur and license returns up-to-date. Frank and the Settlement Manager drove around the village talking into two portable radios that they never did get to work. It was later determined that different frequencies had been assigned to each radio rendering them useless. The plan had been to leave one of the radios in the Hunting Camp on Coats Island for emergency use. Frank and Lorne finally gave up in frustration and we went to Stevenson's house for supper. The Christmas tree lit up the living room and all the lights in the windows were blinking. Three excited children scampered about. I thought of my own family and wondered what they would be doing this evening. I felt like I was on the other side of the world, separated from all those whom I knew and loved. I wondered if I would make it out for Christmas.

Early next morning we headed out to the airstrip. We wanted to lift off as soon as it was light enough to ensure the longest possible daylight hours would be available. The southeast lightened with a pale white glow as Don applied power and started his take-off roll.

Morning dawned clear as we set a course south to Coats Island. Southampton and Native Bay were white with land-fast ice, but soon we reached the floe-edge. The dark water of Fisher Strait began to slip beneath us. Small pans of ice speckled the sea below, but I noted there was more water than ice-pans.

66

'Those ice-pans aren't big enough to land on anyway,' I thought. 'If that engine quits, we won't have a chance.' I turned away from the window and looked over at Frank and Lorne and then at the pile of freight and mail that was destined for the Inuit Camp. 'I wonder if it's really such a big deal to them?' I thought to myself. I recalled that they had gone over in a 'Longliner' boat the previous August prepared to stay for a full year.

'It probably wouldn't be such a big disappointment if we didn't come. They take life day by day; I'd be surprised if they even know we are coming. Lorne must have promised them he'd come or something.' These and other thoughts coursed through my anxious brain as I gazed down at the ice-speckled black water below. The thought that we would soon have to retrace this flight path stabbed my guts like a knife. If the engine failed I wondered what the final minutes would be like.

The plane was once again over land-fast ice and soon we were flying along the north coast of the island looking for the camp. The camp was invisible under the drifted snow, but we spotted the beached 'Longliner' and knew the camp was nearby. Don began circling looking for a relatively smooth spot to touch down. It was a much better landing than at Scottie's camp; the snow was much softer and deeper here. Don faced the Otter into the wind and adjusted the throttle so it would idle.

'I'm not shutting it down!' he yelled. 'You've got one hour to do your business!'

No one argued, most certainly not me. I had visions of the aircraft not starting and all of us being stranded. We started to unload while Stevenson headed off to locate the camp.

The camp consisted of shack-tents which had been walled up with snow blocks initially and were now largely drifted over. The porches were made of snow-blocks much like the entrance to an igloo. There were three or more separate dwellings. The inside was arranged similar to the traditional igloo with a large sleeping shelf. The interiors were heated, not by the *akudliks* or soapstone lamps but by a small oil heater. The fuel had been brought over on the boat.

The families consisted of women and children. The men were out hunting at the floe edge. Lorne was anxious to make contact with the hunters and tried to find out where they were hunting. Then he asked Don if he would consider flying over where they were.

'It all depends on how rough the area looks,' Don said reluctantly. 'I'm not going to spend Christmas on Coats Island if I can help it.'

Everything was unloaded and delivered to the women and children in the huts. They were not warmly dressed but then, I thought, they stay indoors all the time anyway.

The camp had food in abundance. Seal, walrus for the dogs, and caribou.

They were allowed to take a small quota, but caribou had not yet multiplied greatly since their transplant back to the island. Weather conditions and over-hunting had eliminated the animals in years previous.

The people were genuinely happy to see us and to get mail and news from relatives in Coral Harbour. We wished them well and departed.

We skirted the floe-edge and located the hunters without difficulty. The land-fast ice was smooth and we managed to land close by. The hunters came over to talk to us. They were magnificently dressed in full caribou clothing and their *kamiks* (slippers which fit over their double hair-in, hair-out caribou stockings) were made of polar bear fur. What a contrast to their rag-tag families back in the huts. These were the hunters who spend every waking hour outside procuring food for their families. These hunters probably looked as their ancestors looked when the first *Qallunnaaq* (or white-man) made contact with them.

Don got the Otter back in the air without incident and headed back to Coral Harbour. I took a deep breath and whispered a fervent prayer as we drifted out over the black water of Fisher Strait once again. 'It would seem so cruel if I were never to see my wife and soon-to-be born child now after all the long weeks of waiting.'

The wheel skis thudded down on the runway at Coral Harbour as I gave a huge sigh of relief. So far things had gone well for us. Now we had another night to rest before we started the long flight to Churchill.

On Tuesday, 23 December we left Coral Harbour, planning to make Churchill by supper-time. I was secretly hoping we would arrive before the Transair Mainliner left for Winnipeg. I didn't have a reservation and I expected the plane to be packed with Christmas travelers but I held out a faint hope of a last minute cancellation that would put me on my way south.

Our flight progressed well until we reached Rankin Inlet in the early afternoon. There was a delay in getting fuel for the aircraft and before we were ready to go again two hours had elapsed. I looked at my watch as we set a course for Churchill. 'There's no way we'll make it in before Transair leaves,' I thought. 'It's probably fully booked anyway.' I resigned myself to staying in Churchill that night.

When our wheels touched the runway in Churchill there was exactly thirty minutes left before the Mainliner was due to leave. The strong north wind had helped us out for a change, pushing us in ahead of schedule. I could see the YS–11 Turbo-prop sitting outside the Transair Terminal as we pulled up in front of Lambair's hanger.

I grabbed Frank's arm. 'I'm going to run over and see … there just might be a chance I could get on.' I caught my breath. 'If I do get on, can you manage everything here?'

'Don't worry about things here; go and see, you might be lucky.'

'Thanks, Frank,' I said as I vaulted to the door and started running for the terminal.

The place was packed and my hopes of getting on plummeted. 'Well, I'm here, I may as well ask,' I thought as I hurried up to the ticket counter.

'Any chance of a vacant seat?' I queried as soon as the agent looked up.

'Well this must be your lucky day,' he replied. 'I just put down the phone. There's a cancellation. I think we have a seat for you.'

'One way to Winnipeg then, please,' I said as I began to dig into my bush-clothes for a credit card. By the time I had my ticket and boarding pass they were calling the flight. I was still dressed in down-filled wind-pants, parka and fur hat but I didn't care, there was no way I was going to take time to change clothes now. I got in the line-up heading out the door.

I just couldn't believe my good fortune. When I got to Winnipeg, I checked for flights going to Saskatoon and got on an extra section leaving at 3 a.m. By 5 a.m. I was getting a rent-a-car guy in Saskatoon out of bed and by 6 a.m. I was on the road north to Prince Albert. Before 9 a.m. I was knocking on my brother's door and holding Iris in my arms once more. It was still difficult to believe I had come so far without a reservation the day before Christmas.

At least Iris hadn't had the baby yet. Our reunion was special and that Christmas a memorable one. The baby was overdue but seemed in no hurry to be born, so we enjoyed the next eight days of waiting visiting friends and family.

When our son did arrive at 3:30 p.m. on 3 January, it was after Iris had endured 21 hours of labour but she managed a groggy smile after the delivery. I was glad she was in competent care. I went down to see our new son through the glass and there I stood with tears in my eyes for a long time just looking at our little boy. I was now part of a little miracle and my head was full of thoughts which only a new father is capable of dreaming as he looks upon his child for the first time.

It was eight days before Iris was released from hospital. It was a rough time, but her courage never failed and soon we were heading to her home in Assiniboia, Saskatchewan. She would spend time with her parents while I began the long trip back to our home in Baker Lake. My holiday time had expired and I needed to get back to my job. Another parting; another farewell. It never seemed to get any easier no matter what the circumstances.

CHAPTER FIFTEEN

At Home – But Not for Long

Hear how it whispers like voices I know
Lost in the pale of the morning.

Only The Wind

SUNDAY, 25 JANUARY was my birthday so I planned to sleep late. The wind awakened me around 9 a.m. and I lay quietly listening to the incessant moaning over the roof and around the corners of the house. Perhaps another storm was building.

The winter of 1970 had been extremely cold and stormy. Some older Inuit friends had confirmed it. My weeks alone had been difficult at times but in a way I was glad Iris and our little son were safe with her parents in Saskatchewan, far away from the cold and storms of the Keewatin.

The phone disturbed my thoughts and comfort as I reluctantly crawled out of bed to answer it. The Air-radio operator was on the line.

'Good morning. I have a radiogram for you.'

'Go ahead and read it please,' I said.

'It reads: Happy Birthday, I'll be coming home on Wednesday's flight. Love, Iris.'

I thanked the operator and hung up the phone. I noticed that the large window in the living room was almost drifted up with snow. Only a few inches at the top remained clear. I went over and looked out. The nearest houses were barely visible through drifting clouds of snow. The sun had not yet risen.

'Another stormy day,' I thought. 'I hope things improve before Wednesday.' I turned away and began to think about breakfast.

By Monday morning the wind had lessened but it was very cold. I pulled on my caribou *kulituuk* or outer parka over my other clothes and set out for the office. My first breath of cold air made me gasp. The wind cut my face and I could feel my cheeks begin to freeze. I held my caribou mitten against my face as I covered the short distance to the office building. I ducked into the ice-porch and opened the main door.

Gerry Tanner was the only one in the office. The building felt cool despite the constant humming of the furnace.

'It feels really cold this morning,' I said to Gerry as I came in his office.

'It's minus 54 degrees with a 25 kph wind,' he replied. 'I just phoned Air-radio.'

'So what are we doing here?' I asked as I pulled off my *kulituuk*.

'Good question,' Gerry replied. 'There won't be much moving today.'

Nothing moved for several days as the temperature hovered near minus 50 degrees. I looked at my wind-chill chart on the wall. It went beyond the highest reading listed.

On Wednesday, Transair canceled the scheduled flight because of the extreme temperatures. By Thursday the wind had dropped and the temperature crept up to the minus 40-degree range. We were advised that Transair would be in around 2 o'clock. I had talked to Iris in Churchill the previous day so I was expecting her on the flight.

I drove the Bombardier to the ice strip and waited for the plane. Iris arrived with little Kevin on her back inside her warm *amoutik*. Soon we were inside our home once again. Unfortunately our happiness was to be of short duration. Two days after arriving home, Kevin became sick. He couldn't keep anything in his tiny stomach. Thinking perhaps it was due to the stress of travel, Iris tried patiently to nurse him, but he continued to vomit every time he was fed. His constant crying was wearing us both down with worry. We both felt so helpless. Iris had been in touch with the nurses and they told us to bring him to the Nursing Station. As I warmed up the Bombardier I noticed the wind had increased again and the air was white with ground-drift. What a cruel winter this was. If only the storm would hold off until we could get a plane in.

The call went out for a 'medi–vac', but we learned the weather was out in Churchill and no planes were flying. Iris stayed at Kevin's side all day Sunday and through the next night. It was heartbreaking to see our little boy with intravenous tubes in both legs. He cried incessantly and there was nothing we could do to relieve his suffering.

The weather was still out on Monday. Iris could hardly speak without crying. The strain of the last 48 hours was so evident on her face. It all seemed so unfair. To be together for so short a time, and now watching our baby fight for his life. Our constant prayer was for a break in the weather so a plane could get in.

On Tuesday, 3 February, the Air-radio operator was able to contact a DC3 in the air out of Yellowknife and en route to Uranium City. The weather had improved enough in Baker Lake for a plane to land and was marginal but improving in Churchill. The pilot of the DC3 agreed to divert to Baker Lake for the medical emergency.

Iris wearing Inuit amoutik with baby on back.

In early afternoon the sound of an aircraft could be heard. Relief swept over us like a wave as the plane circled the ice strip. The plane landed and twenty-six passengers got off. Nora, the nurse, Iris and our baby got on. In minutes the plane was skimming down the ice runway and climbing into the clear sky. I watched as it set a course for Churchill and disappeared in the haze.

What occurred after the plane left will always be remembered as one of the finest examples of northern kindness and hospitality I will ever witness. Twenty-six total strangers were approached by our friends and neighbours and whisked away to homes where they were looked after until their charter aircraft could return and pick them up. Not one word of complaint was heard about their inconvenience. We will never forget the kindness and support we received from the community that day.

In Churchill Iris would have a tearful confrontation with a doctor who hadn't bothered to read the nurse's diagnosis. She was worried that any delay could result in missing the Transair flight to Winnipeg for emergency surgery. Eventually things began to get sorted out and Kevin made the flight to Winnipeg. Iris returned to Baker Lake exhausted but relieved that her baby was in good care.

It was almost two weeks before we would have our boy with us again. He was due to be sent home on one flight but when we met the plane, he was not on it. Someone in Churchill had missed getting him and the escort on the flight.

Finally on 18 February we met the Transair flight and Iris scooped our baby in her arms. Tears traced her cheeks as she folded back the blankets for a peek. It was Kevin all right; he had a slight cold but managed a smile for us. I thanked the lady who had accompanied him on the flight. We climbed in the Bombardier and headed down the lake. Our family was home and together once again.

CHAPTER SIXTEEN

Celebrating a Centennial

Baker Lake is the village ten men left that day
They said their good-byes and were soon on their way.

Expedition Song

ARLY IN 1970, the Territorial Government in Yellowknife began to make elaborate plans to celebrate the purchase of Rupert's Land and the North-Western Territory from the Hudson's Bay Company. On 21 February, community representatives from every settlement were flown to Yellowknife for a big planning session. The idea was to create a lot of excitement and generate interest in developing a community project. Plans were made to haul the mail by dog team over almost forgotten routes, retrace the old Dawson Patrol from Fort McPherson to Dawson City, Yukon and many other similar projects. In other words, do something outstanding in the spirit of the early explorers. It was almost March and nothing much was being planned for Baker Lake.

It was Ed Zawruycha, the RCMP Corporal, who threw out the first idea to spark interest. He suggested a group of ten should cross the barren-lands by snowmobile and arrive in Yellowknife in time to take in the huge celebrations that were being planned for the city's annual Caribou Carnival. A community meeting was called and there was a great deal of interest in the idea. Ed figured he could persuade the Bombardier Company to provide the snowmobiles free of charge. To everyone's surprise the Company supported the idea and air freighted ten new 18 hp Olympic 335 snowmobiles to the settlement. Planning for the trip began in earnest.

The first setback came when the community received word from the Centennial Committee in Yellowknife which administered the grant money, that our proposal would not be approved. Their reasons, when stripped of political double-talk, amounted to: 'We don't think you will be able to make it. It's never been done before.' Their reply just got everyone mad and more determined than ever. Another community meeting was held and the Baker Lake Residents' Association voted to back the project. We

Leaving Baker Lake for Yellowknife.

would thumb our noses at those Centennial wimps in Yellowknife when we got there. Planning for the trip continued and the Centennial Committee was duly advised that we didn't need their help.

The Commissioner of the Northwest Territories got wind of our plans and thought it was a great idea. He would be in Baker Lake to see us off on 2 April.

When I awoke that morning and heard the wind over the drifts, roof-high around the house, I knew it wasn't a good day for travel. But Commissioner Hodgson was in town to see us off and of course everything had to give way to protocol. So we headed off into cutting winds and blowing snow, searching for that imaginary trail westward to Great Slave Lake and Yellowknife. It would have made more sense to go back home until there was a break in the weather.

The Arctic wind whipped the ground-drift into a white fog as I peered around the hood of my caribou parka at the outline of the komatik ahead. My mind struggled with the many details of the trip. Had we included every essential item of equipment? Would we have enough fuel to get to Fort Reliance? I tried to anticipate what we might encounter in those seemingly endless miles which now stretched before us.

The first ten miles were lost in a swirl of snow ahead and behind. In order to stay together in the blinding snow it was necessary to crowd right up behind the komatik directly ahead. This created a small chain reaction when one of the drivers released the throttle momentarily for one reason or another and the outfit behind swung to the right or left to avoid running into the heavily loaded sled.

It wasn't long until carburetors began to freeze up from ingesting too much powdered snow. Stops were frequent and when one of the party did not catch up immediately, Ed was off on the back trail to see what had happened. This irked me more than it should have, and as I sat on my snowmobile in the swirling snow I tried to analyze my feelings.

Beside the obvious waste of gas, I decided that it was the leadership question which really irritated me. Throughout the planning, the question of an expedition leader was inadvertently brushed aside, to avoid hurting anyone's feelings, it seemed. It was to be a cooperative effort, someone had said, and yet in the back of my mind I knew that out here on this vast unforgiving sea of whiteness someone had to 'call the shots'. It wasn't difficult to identify my problem as simple human pride although it would be some time before I could really deal with it. In the meantime I determined to put forward my best effort and try not to let my feelings spoil the trip.

Ed and Harold emerged from the swirling snow and after a few minutes we decided to push on. Another 30 km or so was gained with repeated stops to clean frozen carburetors. Finally almost all ten machines were acting up so it was decided to stop and wait for the wind to drop. We were near the northeast shore of Pitz Lake about 64 km west of the settlement.

I had a double-wall sail-silk tent which had weathered many storms successfully and it didn't take long to set it up. We protected the walls with large blocks of snow, then retreated inside to light the Coleman stove. As we sat sipping hot mugs of tea, the wind raged against the tent with increased fury.

For a long time we sat in silence; lost in thought. I began thinking of my wife and our four-month-old son. Parting had been particularly painful for me, for I couldn't help wondering how they would manage if I didn't make it back. I was just getting to know my boy again after his long absence in a southern hospital. Would I ever see them again? I knew there would be risk involved; out here even the most experienced traveler could get into serious trouble quickly. Thoughts like these must somehow be suppressed. I was now fully committed and should now focus my mind on the land beyond the western horizon and the arduous trip which lay before me.

After tea, Luke Tunguak and James Ookpuga began constructing two igloos adjacent to the tent in which to shelter for the night. How deftly their flashing snowknives rendered the drift into uniform snow blocks.

How quickly the walls spiraled upward to completion, despite the howling wind. The others carried blocks and chinked the cracks with snow. Now everyone was comfortably prepared to spend the first night on the land. It was time for supper.

The delicious aroma of Arctic hare wafted out through the tent flaps where Gerry Tanner had put together our first meal of the trip. Father Choque, the Catholic priest, had presented us with the meat as a parting gift. Tonight we would feast on sumptuous stew and in our cups, instead of the usual tea, we drank white wine so cold the ice crystals rattled against our teeth. We drank to success. It seemed a fitting gesture for this adventurous undertaking.

The storm continued unabated throughout the night and ushered in the next day. The sky was clear but the wind kept visibility almost at zero. It would be foolhardy to try traveling in these conditions. Time passed slowly and painfully as we sat in our shelters listening to the language of the wind.

By afternoon everyone began to feel the need to be doing something that would prepare us for the big push when the wind would finally subside.

Before long a snowmobile was hauled inside the tent. The carburetor was cleaned, re-installed and covered to keep out the snow. Everyone pitched in and soon each machine was serviced, fueled and ready for the trail.

As the day wore on, we waited, drinking copious quantities of tea, which necessitated frequent excursions outside to 'check the weather'. As evening came I could hear Tunguak talking softly in Inuk-tit-tuut. He was saying something about the weather and when I cast an inquiring glance in his direction he said in his few words of English, 'Soon wind sleeping.' Yes, he was right, for as the sun began its eternal decline toward the hazed horizon, the wind began to slacken.

As twilight settled on our camp white clouds of snow drifted by like huge shadows borne on the ever-weakening wind. Off to the southwest, the dark hulk of an esker began to appear intermittently as the wind began to 'sleep'. Soon all had sought the comfort of bedrolls. The wind whispered around the tent, rustling the silk in gentle rhythmic waves that finally soothed us to sleep.

Morning dawned perfectly calm and clear. The sun was just over the horizon when the camp began to stir. Gerry Tanner shared the tent with me and his first order of business was to take the temperature inside; a chilly minus 28°C. I mentioned that often it's better if you don't know how cold it is. I beat the frost off my bedroll and packed it up. Soon the gas stove began to take the chill off and the others who had slept in the igloos began to crawl in.

Breakfast was hurried affair, the remains of the stew, bannock with jam, all washed down with several cups of hot tea. When everything was stowed, down came the tent and the komatiks were loaded. In minutes we were on our way west, to the trapping cabin at Mary Lake.

We had some trouble getting over a steep ridge and it was necessary to use two machines to get our sleds to the top. It became clear early on that Bill Wilson's snowmobile was using far too much fuel. He always ran his tank dry long before anyone else. We resolved to put the spare carburetor on his machine as soon as we got to the cabin.

The cabin at Mary Lake had been erected the previous winter to serve as a base camp for trapping in this area. I had made many trips by Bombardier snowmobile and sled to bring all the material from Baker Lake, 136 km away. It stood on a large horseshoe shaped island in the middle of the lake.

This was also the site of one of our main fuel caches. With the help of Barnabus Peryouar, I had hauled 270 gallons of fuel here in March, returning in a howling blizzard. I shuddered at the remembrance.

The dark square outline of the cabin appeared on the distant bleak shoreline and a short time later ten snowmobiles towing heavy, lunging komatiks roared up and stopped. In minutes everyone was busy unpacking the sleds, thankful that at least for one night we would have the relative comfort of this lonely cabin.

April 5 dawned clear with a brisk north wind. In the Keewatin region the north wind was an ever-present winter companion. It would be our compass for several more days until we were much further west. Here long fragile fingers of drifting snow, sculptured endless ice-ridges and pinnacles, perfectly aligned with Polaris. We all knew that travel would be grueling across these contrary drifts.

A curious band of caribou circled the cabin as we were preparing to leave. They seemed to know they were quite safe for no one at this point could carry another pound of weight. The 380 gallons of fuel had been distributed evenly and this along with the rest of the supplies had grossly overloaded the komatiks. The caribou disappeared over a low ridge as we started our machines and began to pick our way slowly westward through a maze of rock-hard drifts.

CHAPTER SEVENTEEN

The Point of No Return

With the northwind blowing and fifty below
With a wave of the hand they were off on the land
With a long way to go.

Expedition Song

OUR ROUTE LED ACROSS MALLERY LAKE, north of the Kunwak River, to Tebesjuak Lake. Here we were plagued with innumerable pressure ridges which greatly impeded our progress. Even in the open areas the hard snow ridges reduced our forward speed.

The sun was already setting as we completed the 30 km crossing of the lake and began to search for a suitable campsite. We were 104 km from the cabin and everyone was dead-tired. We finally stopped on a small river about 12 km west of the lake. Northwest of our camp was a long winding esker behind which the pale, orange glow of the departed sun was quickly fading.

On the following day our party made excellent progress, mostly over land, crossing the Dubawnt River at Grant Lake. We then swung northwest for a few kilometers just south of Chamberlin River, to pick up the large unnamed lake on which a fuel cache had been placed.

It was fairly easy to locate for a prominent esker terminated right at the lakeshore, marking the place. We had come about 80 km from our last camp. It was late afternoon when we arrived.

Stopping our snowmobiles, everyone rolled off on the snow to rest in our caribou clothing for a few minutes before setting up camp.

With supper over, everyone gathered in my tent to discuss our situation. This was to be our last cache until Fort Reliance. It was quite possible that we would not have enough to make it with ten machines if fuel consumption remained at present levels.

This was the point of no return. We had to decide now whether to continue or to turn back to Baker Lake. Everyone was asked individually to express his opinion. As I sat mulling things over I thought again of home. Back there was everything that gave life meaning: my wife, my little son. Ahead stretched the unknown: bone-jarring kilometers of snowdrifts, pressure ridges, rocks, bad ice and open water. Who could know what might happen? But I couldn't go back; not without first giving it an honest effort.

As everyone spoke in turn, it was apparent that all wanted to push on as far west as 310 gallons of fuel would take us. Luke Tunguak expressed it very well, with David Owingayak interpreting when he said, 'I shook hands and said good-bye to too many people to go back home now.' The consensus was to push on. No one lingered over tea once agreement was reached. Bedrolls were prepared and soon the camp slept.

The morning temperature in the tent was announced as a cool minus 30°C. The weather was good with light northerly winds. Everyone was in good humour and eager to be off. The morning preparations were already falling into an efficient routine. By nine o'clock we had left our bleak camp behind as we strung ourselves out in a long line heading west.

The sun reflected brightly off the crusted snow and it was soon necessary to protect our eyes with dark glasses. No one wanted to suffer the agony of snow blindness.

The land remained relatively level for many kilometers but soon undulations became common with large boulder-strewn areas. It became necessary to skirt the edges or slowly pick our way through. As the land began to rise, rocky outcroppings crowned many ridges jutting boulders up through the snow. Progress was at times very slow and treacherous.

By midday we had reached the slopes of the Retort River valley where we called a halt. Getting down to the river would be a difficult and dangerous undertaking. Each one would have to find his own way down the steep incline. For many kilometers in each direction the riverbanks were rugged and very steep. We picked what looked like a fairly smooth route and started down.

My descent began slowly as I scanned the snow for hidden boulders. Gradually the heavy sled, unrestrained at the end of the long towrope, began to gather speed and overtake me. I tried to pick a safe track down, maintaining control by spurting ahead to tighten the towrope; thereby changing the direction of the plunging komatik.

Halfway down everything was flying along at breakneck speed. I could do little more than keep ahead of the komatik. The snowmobile shot over the drifts, momentarily airborne, as I approached the run-out at the bottom. Finally everything coasted to a stop. I switched off the engine and let out a whoop. This had been a wild, exciting and dangerous few minutes, which I would not soon forget.

Matthew Koonungnat had made it down just a little before me and he ran over laughing, pointing up the slope where the others were just beginning the descent.

We watched as the rest of the party made the thrilling run to the river. Everyone made it intact. There was some good-natured banter as we recounted the details of our particular experiences coming down the hill.

Our attention soon shifted to the opposite slope. How would we ever get up with our heavy loads? The west side looked almost as steep as the side we had just descended.

We followed the river for several kilometers, seeking the best route to the top. Eventually we stopped at the bottom of a long but relatively even incline. It would be necessary for everyone to gather speed and make an individual run to the top. In this way, if someone became bogged down he would not obstruct others following behind. We visually selected a route and gunned the engines.

Actually it was better than anticipated. One or two machines spun out and had to wait for help but most made it on the first attempt.

Our adrenaline levels returned to normal as the flat, featureless tundra immediately west of the river passed uneventfully beneath the skis.

About 38 km west of the Retort River, the land began to rise again. Some of the truncated hills rose to 390 meters above sea level providing welcome relief from the bleak region just traversed.

As another day faded into soft lingering twilight our party sought refuge near a steep ridge which seemed to emerge suddenly from the upland plain. It was the eastern slope of another esker that snaked away to the southwest as far as I could see in the failing light.

Slowly a camp took shape, bringing a sense of security to an otherwise hostile landscape. As we finished supper talk turned to the day ahead. I hoped we would strike the Clarke River early in the day as I guessed it to be approximately 64 km to the southwest. With the experience of the Retort Valley still fresh in our minds, we all wondered what to expect on the slopes of the Clarke.

Ten weary travelers again sought the solace of warm sleeping robes. Outside the undulating walls of the tent, the ceaseless wind sifted a feathery ground-drift southward over the corrugated surface of the snow to spend its strength in the stunted spruce of the tree line.

CHAPTER EIGHTEEN

Searching for a River

Who could tell of the danger the travelers would face
In that cruel biting wind and the fast grueling pace.

Expedition Song

THE NEXT MORNING during breakfast I learned that Harold Etegoyok had lost his sleeping bag somewhere on the trail west of Tebesjuak Lake. To make matters worse, his wallet was in the same bag. He was now poorer by 75 dollars!

This was the result of carelessness in lashing the canvas on the komatik. The constant bouncing did the rest. It was a hard lesson for he would spend the remainder of the nights sleeping in his caribou clothing. I remembered the long delay when the fringe of his caribou parka was sucked into the open throat of his snowmobile carburetor. Hopefully Harold's luck would start to improve.

Wednesday 8 April dawned clear and cold with an ever-present north wind. The temperature stood at minus 34°C. It was a perfect day for travel and everyone worked quickly and efficiently to break camp. The komatiks were soon packed and tightly lashed. Everyone was anxious to be off.

I enjoyed working with Matthew Koonungnat. He was usually on the point, picking the best trail. Matthew and I had traveled a lot together and I appreciated his abilities on the land.

He was with me as I took the usual compass reading prior to departure. I swung my arm around on the bearing we should follow. Matthew laughed, nodded his head in acknowledgment and off we went once again.

Several uneventful hours passed as we made steady progress through gentle rolling hills and many winding eskers. The bright morning sun disappeared under heavy cloud and before long we were in near white-out conditions.

This made travel extremely dangerous. What might appear as a shallow depression in the snow could be a ten-foot embankment.

Our progress slowed and finally Koonungnat stopped. I thought it was due to deteriorating conditions but David Owingayak, interpreting for the other, pointing across the ravine said in hushed tones, 'There's a herd of muskoxen over there.' Sure enough, a small group of dark shaggy shapes stood placidly on the foggy hillside.

'Let's get closer and take some pictures,' someone suggested. This seemed like a logical thing to do since the muskoxen were just standing there looking at us.

We were drawing closer to the herd and now the animals began to look a little strange. I began to feel a bit foolish. I was sure the others shared my feelings for there, clumped on the side of the slope, were a dozen or more small spruce trees!

Everyone began veering back to our old trail. No one stopped to talk. The 'muskoxen' which mysteriously turned into trees was a subject never again mentioned for the duration of the trip.

It became evident that this was to be a day with more than the usual amount of excitement for later that afternoon we happened on three caribou being harassed by a pair of wolves.

At this point in the trip we needed fresh meat. We decided to take one caribou and distribute the weight between the sleds.

James Ookpuga and Luke Tunguak began to stalk the caribou. At the noise of the approaching snowmobiles the wolves had vanished. The caribou curiously milled about a short distance away. I saw Ookpuga kneel and heard one shot but I could hardly believe my eyes for there were two caribou thrashing about on the snow.

Because I was a Game Management Officer, I was somewhat irritated as I approached the men. I was responsible for ensuring that meat was not wasted and all other game laws were adhered to on the trip. Thinking that Tunguak had also shot and I just hadn't heard it, I asked him rather testily.

'Why did you shoot?'

Tunguak protested, 'Me no shoot; kill two one shot.'

It was just as he said. As the shot was fired, the second caribou wheeled around into the path of Ookpuga's bullet. We were amazed at the occurrence and there was a lot of good-natured joshing as Ookpuga was congratulated.

The caribou were quite thin and when they were skinned and cut up I was relieved to see that all the edible meat could be taken on the komatiks. Before long everything was safely lashed, the machines refueled and we were heading west once again.

By five o'clock that afternoon we were standing on the northeast bank of the Clarke River. We studied the slope carefully for an easy way down. It would be a replay of our experience on the Retort River.

The route down was selected with care and everyone exercised skill in getting his outfit to the river intact. In spite of precautions there were anxious moments when Bill Wilson's komatik got ahead of his snowmobile, nearly spearing Gerry Tanner's machine with one of the runners.

A pleasant camp was pitched between clumps of stunted spruce. Suitable snow was found nearby so our Inuit friends decided to build an igloo. I set about gathering some firewood. I had an idea that fresh caribou ribs roasted over the open fire would be quite appetizing to ten hungry men.

The ribs were suspended beside the fire from a tripod constructed of small poles. The rope holding the meat is twisted then released. This causes the ribs to spin slowly beside the hot coals. I learned this from some Indian friends in the Mackenzie Mountains. Obviously I must have missed something important as the ribs turned out half-cooked and as tough as shoe leather!

After supper everyone rested, drank endless cups of tea and enjoyed the wood fire. Several hours passed and the Inuit members decided to climb the steep hillside just north of the camp for a look around. They took caribou skins with them which they sat on for a rather exhilarating 'magic carpet ride' to the bottom.

As we were preparing to leave early next morning it was thrilling to hear a large wolf pack serenading on the river hills south of the camp. Some movement on the riverbank caught my attention and through field glasses I watched several wolves come down the slope in pursuit of a small band of caribou which moments before had been feeding peacefully on the hillside.

We followed the Clarke River for a distance as we sought a way out of the valley. We were fortunate to find a coulee which led us to the top without incident.

Not many kilometers southwest of the river the land became rocky and rugged, slowing our progress and causing delays. Boogie springs snapped on exposed rocks and carburetors required periodic servicing.

Bill Wilson was working on his machine when Boris Kotelewetz and I stopped to help. The rest went on ahead and disappeared behind a ridge. We worked as quickly as we could and soon had the engine running again.

'Let's get out of here,' Boris shouted over the roar of the engines.

As I looked around at the several forlorn, wind-beaten little spruce trees and the bleak empty terrain and felt the crushing loneliness of this particular place, it seemed like a very appropriate thing to do!

By mid-afternoon, a dark irregular smudge appeared in the distance. Soon we could discern spruce trees staggered along the shallow riverbank. We were approaching the Thelon River.

James Ookpuga, who was leading, swung into a small clearing in the trees and promptly became bogged down in soft, waist-deep snow. Because I was behind Ookpuga, I tried to turn out to the left but I too became hopelessly stuck. The others, who were further back, saw the danger and stopped.

What followed were several hours of intense physical exertion before we were all safely down on the ice of the Thelon River. We were so exhausted and thirsty that we lay for a long time near a clear patch of ice, chipping pieces to suck, unable to wait until a kettle could be boiled.

CHAPTER NINETEEN

Thelon River Camp

Endless hours not knowing the dangers ahead
With the wind for a friend just around the next bend
And the snow for a bed.

Expedition Song

A COMFORTABLE CAMP was established near the east bank of the river. As supper was being prepared, Ed and David approached me to ask if I was certain that this was the Thelon River. I was taken aback when David told me that Tunguak and Ookpuga were saying that this was not the Thelon. They had seen it at Beverly Lake and the banks were much higher. Ed also questioned whether or not this could be some other river.

At first I was somewhat shaken by this apparent uncertainty and didn't know what to say. I was sure we were camped on the Thelon but I certainly couldn't prove it.

I got my maps and with David translating, tried to explain the route we had followed. I explained that the riverbanks were different because we were much further south. No one argued with me but as we went in the tent for supper I knew there were still some serious doubts.

I gave our estimated position as 63 degrees 15 minutes north by 104 degrees, 41 minutes west. This seemed to check out and yet one thing bothered me. Why had it taken longer than anticipated to cross over from the Clarke River? We must have drifted further south than planned.

Next morning we assessed our remaining fuel. We had 110 gallons. Ed announced that he would take Tunguak and Ookpuga and push on to Fort Reliance. Once there, he would arrange for the RCMP Otter aircraft to make a fuel drop at our camp. There didn't seem to be much room for discussion. Ed was the RCMP member of the expedition so he seemed to be the logical one to make these arrangements.

I had rather strong feelings on who should go and who should stay but I decided to keep silent. I was somewhat disappointed that I had not been asked to go with them. Perhaps all three lacked confidence in my

Thelon River Camp Skidoo expedition.

map-reading; after all, I wasn't sure they even believed we were on the Thelon River.

The three men prepared to leave, taking all the remaining fuel. We wished them well as they headed off across the river. In a matter of minutes they had shrunk to three bobbing black dots in the distance before they disappeared.

The rest of the day was spent fixing up the camp. We constructed a large tee-pee using the canvas from our komatiks for covering. We could use it as a kitchen leaving more sleeping space in the tents.

I cut poles for a radio aerial and marked out a landing strip on the river ice. Others cut a fishing hole and put up the NWT flag. Nothing else remained for us to do but wait.

After ten grueling days on the trail, 11 April was a welcome day of rest. Our faces were in bad shape. Frostbite, wind and sun had taken their toll. At last we had a chance to lick our wounds.

While out ptarmigan hunting Boris experienced the first stages of snow blindness. He had neglected to wear his sunglasses. He made it back to camp but spent the next 24 hours lying in the tent with damp tea leaves on his eyelids.

April 12 passed pleasantly. The weather was warm and sunny so everyone loafed around the camp. The fishing hole was a popular spot and soon we had an ample supply of fresh lake trout to round out our rations.

Matthew was working on something in front of the tents. He sat on his komatik for several hours whittling away. No one bothered him although everyone wondered what he was making. Finally around 4 o'clock Matthew went out to the fishing hole and dipped the 'something' he had been working on in the water. What could it be? All eyes were on him as he walked slowly toward the tents where the rest of us were sitting.

He had a grin from ear to ear as he put his creation to his lips and blew on it. The cry of some animal in distress assailed our ears. Matthew had made a flute, complete with finger holes, mouthpiece and sides tightly bound with fishing line. He blew it several more times. It sounded anything but musical!

We were still outside the tents when we heard an aircraft. The dull roar of a single-engine Otter could be heard north of camp.

'Ed must have made it,' someone said.

I dug out my flare-gun and binoculars. Searching the sky I could see the RCMP Otter straight north of us and heading in our direction. He seemed to be following the river.

As the plane drew closer I fired a flare. Then, seconds later, another. The plane continued on course. He must have seen us! We started our snowmobiles and pointed the headlight in the direction of the plane. Suddenly, not more than a kilometer north of our camp the plane changed course and headed southwest. I fired two more flares with no results. We all watched in amazement as the plane droned away, disappearing on the western horizon.

Why would the pilot turn away from the river? If the boys had made it to Reliance the pilot would have our position on the river.

Perhaps they hadn't made it. We were now overdue. Was it possible that this was a search plane?

Next morning after breakfast I set up the single side-band radio, which I had carefully transported inside my bedroll. I tried calling the Forest Service frequency, 1530 kHz. After several tries I picked up Fort Smith loud and clear. I passed our position and asked them to relay a message to the RCMP. I asked them to tell the Otter pilot that he was very near our camp the previous day just before he changed course and left the river. I gave our position as 63° 15″; 104° 41″. As I closed the radio I could see relief on the faces of my companions. They too were tired of waiting and wanted to get moving again.

We built a signal fire on the ice and waited. By 2 o'clock the solitude of our camp was again shattered by the roar of approaching aircraft. The RCMP Otter landed while an Aztec aircraft buzzed around overhead.

The Otter pilot said he had been trying to locate us for three days. He didn't know the whereabouts of Ed and the other men. They hadn't made it to Fort Reliance. After five days on the trail there was no doubt that now they were in serious trouble.

We unloaded the fuel and the pilot prepared to leave. He said he would search for Ed and the others on the way home. He also asked me to keep a radio schedule with him at 9 p.m.

Soon the plane was airborne and headed over the low ridge where we had watched our companions disappear five days earlier.

I had checked our position on the Thelon River with the pilot. We were camped just south of Eyeberry Lake. Actually I had given our position as being on the Thelon, north of the lake. We were 20 km further south than expected.

After the fuel was mixed and loaded everyone was restless and wanted to travel. We decided to wait until the next day to see if there was any news about Ed and the others.

That night on the radio our fears were confirmed. The pilot had been unable to locate them. They had decided to call in search and rescue.

CHAPTER TWENTY

Lost in Fog and Darkness

We've gone just as far as we ever can go,
Our dogs are all gone, and we're lost in the snow.

Only The Wind

A s THE NEW DAY BEGAN we were ready to leave but after contacting
Fort Smith by radio we were advised to wait in camp for another
aircraft. We didn't need another aircraft but decided to wait. By afternoon
no plane had arrived so we decided to get underway. We planned to follow
Ed's trail for a while and try to determine his direction of travel. Later
we would decide what our next move would be.

As if to convince us that we had overstayed our welcome on the Thelon,
a wide band of floodwater, over a foot deep, began to approach the camp
from the south. We got everything loaded just before the camp flooded. I
had to put on my rubbers in order to retrieve Gerry's twelve-pound lake
trout, which he had buried in the snow.

How good it felt to be traveling once more. For a few miles the trail
took us southwest. Near the Mary Francis River Ed's trail turned south.
We stopped to discuss the situation. If they went very far south they would
intercept the tree line too soon and would have a difficult time in the soft
snow.

We decided to follow the trail for a while longer just to confirm their
apparent direction of travel. I would pass this on to Fort Smith and perhaps
assist search and rescue aircraft.

The trail continued south by southwest toward Whitefish Lake. They
should have been going directly west. There was little doubt this course
would take them into trouble.

We had left the Thelon around 4 p.m. and as nightfall was closing in
we decided to camp. I had a radio schedule to keep with Fort Smith. I
passed the information we had gathered and it was confirmed that Ed and
the others were too far south. The Otter pilot had seen their tracks on

Whitefish Lake. We decided to re-trace our route north to the Mary Francis River and then head due west in the morning.

After we had eaten, Gerry, Bill and Boris were sitting in my tent when someone from the other tent started a snowmobile. Since it was after 11 p.m. we wondered what was going on and stumbled outside.

Matthew was heading south. Further away two lights danced in the distance. Obviously he was off to meet them.

We all stood in stunned silence as the snowmobiles drew up to the tents. It was Tunguak and Ookpuga and riding behind on one of the komatiks was Ed.

It was well past midnight before their stories were told. They had crossed Whitefish Lake then followed the Snowdrift River until finally defeated by soft snow and impassable terrain they decided to return. They had been struggling for five days.

On their way back they passed an igloo used on their outward journey. They were tempted to stop for the night; however they decided to press on and this was the best decision they could have made. Had they not done so, all they would have found the next morning was our empty campsite. They would not have had enough fuel to catch us.

Ed had left his outfit two hours down the trail as he felt the expedition had failed and wanted to save fuel. Bill and Boris agreed to get up early to retrieve it. This would delay our departure but it couldn't be helped. We needed his outfit to complete the trip.

It was 16 April and we were far behind on our travel schedule. I called Fort Smith and asked them to call off the search.

By 11 a.m. we were backtracking north to the Mary Francis River. From there we would head directly west across Tyrrell Lake on route to a fuel cache that we had established near Crystal Island on Artillery Lake.

Throughout the day we drove westward as fast as terrain and conditions would permit. We were anxious to make up some lost time. Finally fatigue and darkness forced us to camp just south of Williams Lake.

We were up in the early dawn but when we looked outside our spirits fell. The sky was obscure and the surrounding hills were shrouded in fog. It was foolish to think of traveling. Waiting would not be easy either. There is a word in the Inuit language for this situation, *Ajornarmat*, meaning it can't be helped, and we certainly couldn't help the fog to lift.

Time passed slowly. At 3 p.m. the fog had lifted a little so we decided to break camp. I took a compass bearing before we left.

Conditions failed to improve and we had only gone about 13 km when we came to a large lake. The fog closed in again and we were forced to stop.

We sat on our snowmobiles for more than an hour hoping the fog would lift. Instead it seemed to get thicker. Finally the call was made to break out the tents.

Everyone was disgruntled. As David rolled off his snow machine he yelled sarcastically, 'Well, we made our hundred yards for the day anyway.' At the time no one saw any humour in his remark.

Just at dusk I climbed a hill near the lake to keep a radio schedule. Somewhat restless from a day of inactivity, Ed, Gerry and Bill decided to accompany me. It took several minutes to make radio contact. There was a message concerning fuel that the aircraft had dropped for us. Finally I gathered up the aerial and we began descending the hill. During this time, fog and darkness had settled quickly.

We walked along for several minutes when suddenly something seemed strange.

'Hey!' I yelled. 'Are we going in the right direction?'

Everyone stopped. We were suddenly aware that no one was certain of the direction to the camp. Every feature of that barren hillside was now obscure in fog and darkness.

Ed had a flashlight and began to use it to search for our old tracks in the snow. The others also began to search around and we got separated. There was nothing but a confusion of tracks in Ed's flashlight beam as we walked back and forth. We soon lost all sense of direction.

I was near a rock on the windswept side of the ridge and I called to everyone to come to this spot. I was sure if we didn't stay together a bad situation would just become worse.

I tried to sound casual although at this moment I certainly didn't feel so calm. I said something to the effect that in these conditions we could quickly become lost. There was no point walking around in circles if we weren't sure of our directions.

'Let's just sit down here a minute and think this through,' I said as everyone gathered around. We began to discuss our next move.

We thought of swallowing our pride and shouting at the tents for someone to turn on a light. This proved useless because everyone in the tents was now sound asleep and no one heard us. In these open expanses all sound quickly dissipates.

Someone suggested we should try again to retrace our tracks. I said that would be a waste of time since now there were footprints everywhere.

'Unless we are sure of the direction we should stay right here,' I stated emphatically. This didn't go over very well as the others paced around, anxious to try finding the camp. I knew that if we were to become separated in the darkness a tragedy could result.

To pass the time I remember relating a story told to me by Scottie Tooloolee that suddenly came to mind.

As a young man he headed off with his dogs to go to a nearby village. Fog and darkness closed in on him. He lost his sense of direction and stopped. He knew he would have to sit until daylight to go on. After a long time he saw a light flare up nearby, like someone lighting a primus stove. It looked pretty close so he left his dogs and began running towards the light. After a few minutes the light faded and went out. Before long he became disorientated again.

He dug snow up with his hands for shelter and sat down to listen and watch. He spent the whole night there on the snow and as the sky lightened he could make out his dog team asleep on the snow and in the distance he could see the igloo village.

'He was smart to stay put until he could see where he was going,' I said. 'And I think we should do the same.'

I said, 'Look, if we have to spend the night out here it's not the end of the world. It will be daylight soon and we know we are only a little way from the tents.'

Actually, I couldn't think of a more dreary prospect.

The clouds seemed to thin out momentarily and we could see the pale outline of the moon. We tried to get our bearings. We seemed to sense the general direction to the camp. Keeping in voice contact we began to venture out one at a time. One would go a short distance and then stop. The next person went further then stopped keeping in contact by yelling all the while. After several probes outward in various directions, Bill yelled that he thought he could make out the camp.

We followed his voice and when we had gathered he ventured out further. He was sure now that the two dark shapes he could see was the camp. This was encouraging since we knew the tents would be one shape and the other was probably the machines and sleds parked a few meters away.

We decided to walk as a group in the direction of these indistinct shapes. In less than five minutes we were at the tents.

No one spoke; no one lit a lamp. Quickly and quietly we sought our sleeping robes.

This experience was not mentioned at breakfast and like the muskoxen that suddenly became spruce trees, it was never mentioned again during the trip or to my knowledge, any time thereafter.

CHAPTER TWENTY-ONE

Race to Fort Reliance

Over the land now, the white clouds of snow
Slip silently by in the morning.

Only The Wind

APRIL 18 AND WE STILL hadn't made it to Fort Reliance. We should have been in Yellowknife by now. It was clear that out here on the immense barren-land, time and schedules were meaningless.

We made an early start in fine weather and soon many miles lay behind us as we drove relentlessly toward Artillery Lake. We struck a chain of lakes leading west by northwest and for several hours made excellent progress.

When the compass proved unreliable I used Greenwich Mean Time (GMT) and our nearest west longitude to calculate the true bearing of the sun. This helped keep us on track. By late afternoon we followed a small creek to the east shore of Artillery Lake.

A high winding pressure ridge jammed right into shore. I climbed up on it and with binoculars tried to locate the south end of Crystal Island. It was difficult to distinguish the eastern shoreline from the island because of the pressure ridge.

I thought the chain of lakes had taken us too far north and mistook the point at Timber Bay, 8 km down the lake, to be the tip of the island. Consequently we headed south not realizing that we were standing less than 2 km south of our fuel cache.

We camped near the mouth of the Lockhard River. After supper, Matthew, David and I went back up the lake and retrieved the fuel.

It was past midnight when we headed down the lake again. The sky was cloudy and darkness settled on us as we traveled south. The echo of our unmuffled engines reverberated from the rocky shore. We arrived back at camp cold and exhausted from the long day on the trail. Gerry had thoughtfully waited up for us with biscuits and hot tea.

The next morning as we prepared to leave, nine timber wolves trotted past, curiously watching the camp from well out in the lake. The Inuit men walked out on the ice keeping in a tight group, hoping to get close enough for a shot. The wolves watched them approach for a few minutes then scattered. Shots hit the snow around them but none were hit.

We all hoped to be in Fort Reliance that afternoon. It was only 24 km as the crow flies but we expected plenty of trouble following the tortuous route over Pike's Portage and then descending Glacier Creek to Great Slave Lake.

As we left the long southern finger of the lake to begin the portage trouble came early. The lakeshore rose sharply and Ed got his outfit bogged down in soft, deep snow.

Rather than stop right there and chance getting stuck as well, everyone behind just passed by and kept on going. About 2 km further up we stopped to wait for him. Before long we heard his machine approaching. He jumped off, hopping mad. He wanted to know why no one had helped him when he was in trouble.

After several minutes of rather heated exchange between Ed and myself, tempers began to cool and we were able to take to the trail once more. The strain and frustration of seventeen days on the land was beginning to show.

The lead machines reached a chain of lakes and waited for the others to catch up. It was a long wait. Gerry's komatik runner had collided with the track-tightening bolt on Bill's machine and it took some time to repair.

By early afternoon we were poised above a steep 15 meter incline which led down to Glacier Creek. The only way to get down was to unhitch and take the snowmobiles down first. Then with men at the bottom to slow the komatik, each one was lined up carefully at the top then released.

The sled accelerated quickly down the steep embankment and shot out on the ice of the creek. Immediately the men grabbed it, much like one would bulldog a steer, and tried to slow it down before it crashed into the opposite bank.

It was slow and dangerous work but this was the only way to get on the creek. One sled turned sideways and rolled but there was no serious damage. At last we had everything safely down and we prepared our outfits to descend to Great Slave Lake.

Our immediate obstacle was frozen Glacier Creek. It was more like a frozen waterfall than anything else. The incline was steep, rocky and mainly glare ice. In places the ice was dangerously thin with deep air pockets.

We lashed our snowmachines to the side of the komatik for better control. Perhaps the engine would hold things back a little. Slowly, tediously, we headed down. There was little chance of finding a place to stop should we run into trouble. Matthew took the lead and after giving him a head start, I began the descent.

Bill's outfit crashed through the thin ice into an air-pocket two meters deep with knee-deep water at the bottom. He wasn't hurt but it took time to fish everything out.

It was only about two kilometers down to the lake but it took several hours and plenty of hard work to get there. To our disappointment we found that for a long way out from the shore the lake was covered with more than 30 cm of floodwater from the Lockhart River. We hoped for solid ice underneath.

Water or not, we weren't about to stop now. There was Fort Reliance on the point not more than five kilometers distant. Off we went, with water spraying in every direction. By 3:30 p.m. we were pulling up in front of the weather station.

The weather station personnel were very hospitable and we were immediately invited for supper. The mere thought of an ample, professionally prepared meal after seventeen days of tea and pilot biscuits created anticipation. We spent the time until supper repairing our equipment and mixing fuel.

It was without much personal preparation that ten hungry men crowded into the very warm dining area of the station. Most of us had lived in the same clothing for nearly three weeks. With sub-zero temperatures this poses no problem. However, in the extreme warmth of the dining room I became aware of a distinct odour arising from my person. Now I began to understand why the weather personnel, so hospitable and friendly at our entry, were now excusing themselves to attend to various important duties elsewhere. Soon only the cook remained. After serving a delicious steak, he continued to visit, sprinkling his conversation with references to the fine shower facilities available in the building.

Bill Wilson was sitting next to me and finally I said apologetically, 'I hope you stink as bad as I do.' He laughed. Bill had forgotten to bring a lighter parka so had to spend all his time inside a very old, smelly, caribou parka. With the slightest movement it rained hair incessantly into our food and drink. He had suffered many uncomplimentary remarks during the trip. Now he said. 'Don't worry, I can only smell myself so far.'

Relief was apparent on the cook's face as we finished our meal, rendered thanks and left. Later we did accept his offer of a hot shower, and it was a delightful experience. It was almost strange to lie on a real bed again after so many nights in the cold air. The room, even with a window open, seemed oppressively hot.

As comfortable as things were at Fort Reliance, we were eager to be off again; however, we had to do some welding on our machines and most of the next day was spent effecting necessary repairs. Almost all the motor mounts were broken, the result of merciless pounding over rock-hard drifts.

The muffler on my snowmobile had broken off somewhere west of Williams Lake and I traveled the rest of the way with tight wads of tissue stuffed in my ears.

CHAPTER TWENTY-TWO

Across the Big Lake to Yellowknife

When at last it was over in Yellowknife town,
With greetings, handshakes and smiles all around.

Expedition Song

F INALLY AT 4:30 A.M., 21 April we headed out on Great Slave Lake, following the Kahochella Peninsula along the south side of McLeod Bay. Travel conditions were good and we were making excellent progress.

This initial rapid progress was relatively short-lived for the leaders soon noticed that the rest of the party had dropped so far behind we could no longer see them. We stopped and waited for them to catch up. We suspected that someone had trouble at one of the two pressure ridges we had crossed. After a very long wait, everyone finally caught up.

Boris had dropped his snowmobile through thin ice at the first pressure ridge. It could have been very serious. He had to hold on to the back of the seat to keep it from sinking while he hollered for assistance. The others rushed over and helped him pull it out. The fuel tank had to be drained, thus the long delay. We continued again at a steady pace and soon we were approaching a height of land called 'the Gap', which would take us over the peninsula into Christie Bay. This steep treed ridge looked formidable from out in the lake. We drew up at the edge of the ice and stopped.

I asked Matthew if he would drop his komatik and go over for a look. If the crossing proved too tough we would go further down the bay, around a long point then back up again to cross over into Wildbread Bay. Matthew roared off into the trees.

Not many minutes elapsed before he was back. He seemed very excited and was sweating profusely. He pulled off his parka, rolled up his sleeves and muttered, '*Piunngillualuk*,' meaning, 'It is very bad.'

I drove along wondering what had upset Matthew so and how long was he going to drive in the cold air without his parka. We were 8 km or more down the bay before, without stopping, he pulled it on.

The next day I learned from David what had happened at the Gap. Apparently Matthew got stuck in soft snow, and while trying to get turned around he encountered a black bear just out of hibernation, at very close quarters. The bear gave Matthew added incentive to get his snowmobile unstuck and out of the trees without delay.

Travel conditions began to get sticky, owing to the mild sunny weather. Engines began to over-heat and so it was necessary to hold up for a while in Lost Channel.

We took the trail again around 7 p.m. and traveled until well past 11 p.m. We pitched our tents far out on Christie Bay. We had carefully skirted areas of bad ice and open water coming out of Lost Channel and we didn't feel like pushing our luck in poor light conditions.

At 4:30 a.m. we were on the trail again. Numerous pressure ridges slowed us down and sapped a lot of energy. Although everyone was extremely tired we kept traveling until the snow began to get sticky and engines again began to over-heat.

We had difficulty getting around bad ice and open water at Utsingi Point. It was necessary to squeeze right up on the rocky shore, then pick our way carefully around the open water along a narrow ice collar.

By mid-afternoon we were camped again, close to the north shore near Blanchet Island. After supper we were surprised to see a Cessna 180, flying very low, approaching from the west. Ed fired a hand-held flare, which flew into the tent, burning hair off a caribou skin. The second flare worked better and the pilot saw it and landed.

The pilot and his passenger were checking out a route for some mining equipment, which was to be trucked out the next day. We exchanged information and were able to arrange for some needed fuel to be put on one of the trucks.

The plane took off and soon everyone was sleeping soundly. Or so we thought. We later learned that Ookpuga and Tunguak had taken turns guarding the camp all night. Apparently shortly after everyone else had collapsed into his bedroll, these two, who were still drinking tea, heard a commotion in the bush on the shore nearby. Two bears were either fighting or mating and creating quite a racket. Ookpuga and Tunguak, fearing the animals might smell the camp, sat all night peering out through the tent flaps.

By 4:15 a.m. we were moving again, to take advantage of good travel conditions. Everyone wanted to bring our long journey to completion and good progress was made.

Shortly after passing the Caribou Islands, we met the Mine trucks. It was almost 8:00 a.m. They told us were 51 km from Yellowknife. After receiving our fuel we thanked everyone and pushed on.

Before long we were heading northwest toward Yellowknife Bay. We had to slow down a little as the engines began to over-heat again. Twenty kilometers out we met a Federal Fisheries Bombardier and a little further on we met a representative of the Yellowknife Snowmobile Club. By 11:00 a.m. we were at the Indian village of Detah. We pushed on up the bay after a brief stop at the village. Soon we called another halt on the ice in front of Con Mine. Ed climbed the steep rocky shore to reach the Mine Office. He wanted to phone the Centennial Centre and announce our arrival. When he returned he said our official reception was set for 2 p.m. at the Ptarmigan Airways dock.

I looked at my watch. It was just past noon. It would be a difficult wait. We unlashed our komatiks and dug out the last of our meager provisions. We sat on our Skidoos and ate our last lunch on the trail together. We had arrived safely after twenty-two difficult days. We had driven over terrain never crossed by anyone in winter before us. It had been a great adventure.

It was about five kilometers to the Ptarmigan dock. We planned our approach and decorated our machines with little flags and centennial stickers. The large banner we had carried from Baker Lake was unfurled and attached to two tent poles. Big red letters announced: 'Baker Lake to Yellowknife Centennial Skidoo Expedition –70.'

At last it was time to depart. We fired up our noisy machines and headed to the dock. As we approached I could see a large crowd had gathered to greet us. We drove up and stopped in line. The banner was held high. Camera shutters whizzed. Familiar faces emerged from the crowd. Nearby Liz Kotelewetz, Nancy Wilson and Carole Zawyrucha embraced their husbands. Somehow they had managed to get a flight across to Yellowknife.

It was several days before we were able to arrange a DC3 charter to take us home. In the interim activities had been planned for us and the time passed pleasantly. We signed the guest book at city hall right below Princess Alexandra of the Netherlands. We were given an official tour of Giant Gold Mine. We donned miner's gear and were taken deep below the surface. For most of us it was the first time underground.

'*Urquuraalummiik!*' (How very hot it is), Luke Tungwak declared as we started walking up the drift following our tour guide.

It was very hot indeed and smelled of sulfur. Other than our miner's lamps: total blackness. I was thinking we would all be glad to be back on the surface again, especially our Inuit friends.

An official banquet was held the next evening in our honor. We weren't exactly wearing formal attire, but we had cleaned up and bought some new clothes for the occasion.

Our charter aircraft departed for Baker Lake at 4:30 a.m. on 30 April.

Members of the expedition on arrival at Yellowknife.

One side was loaded with our komatiks and gear, and the other had seats. It felt good to be heading home after so many days on the trail. We knew it would be early morning when we arrived and we didn't think many people would be there to greet us. How wrong we were. As the plane landed on the lake ice in front of the community it looked like the whole town had turned out to meet us. I spotted a huge 'Welcome Home' banner held above the crowd. Iris was there with Kevin snug and warm in her *amoutik.*

Everyone wanted to shake hands and congratulate us. It was a bit overwhelming but very gratifying to receive such an outpouring of support from the community. On the walk home over the big familiar snowdrifts, Iris mentioned that the Armed Forces were arriving to conduct a parachute drop on the lake.

'That's nice,' I said. 'We can watch from the roof of our house.' Actually all that really mattered now was to get home and hug my wife and little son once again. As we walked along, a complexity of emotion stirred within me; feelings that only a kindred spirit who had also experienced the immensity of the primordial barren-lands in winter, could truly understand.

CHAPTER TWENTY-THREE

Death Came Softly on the Wind

And still the wind whispers like voices I know
And moans like a widow in mourning.

Only The Wind

S cottie tooloolee was spending the winter of 1971 in his camp at
the south end of Parker Lake. It was his second winter on the land and
I liked to support him as much as I could because of his hunting and
trapping efforts. He was a man probably in his sixties, but it was hard to
know for sure.

He usually took younger men with him on the land and they learned
much from the old man. Barney Sitowak was at his camp for the second
winter. Since it was already mid April and the fox season would close in
two weeks, I expected to see his dog team coming across the lake any day.

A howling Arctic blizzard began Thursday afternoon.

I happened to be in the Game Management office when this particular
storm hit the settlement. I was packing some Arctic fox pelts for shipment
to a southern fur auction, when I glanced out the window. The wind was
whipping up a strong ground drift; a good indication that a storm was on
the way. I noticed some activity down on the lake; a dog team was coming
in. The driver was having difficulty getting his team and heavy komatik
over the high, hard drifts that had accumulated around the settlement
buildings. As the team passed the office, I recognized Scottie Tooloolee as
the driver. I was pleased that the old man had judged the weather so well.
He was now safely home and would have plenty of information for me
about wildlife in that area. I looked forward to having a good chat with
him.

The storm raged through the weekend and by Sunday afternoon the
wind had dropped somewhat. I was at the office as usual on Monday
morning when old Scottie came in with a worried look on his face. He
began immediately to relate something to Barnabus in an excited tone of

voice. Barnabus, my Inuit assistant, spoke understandable English. At least I could understand him and that was what really mattered.

'*Sunali una*,' I asked Barnabus after Scottie had stopped talking.

'He say, maybe Michael Alerk and Barney Sitowak skidoo break, no coming, maybe stuck.'

It took a while to get the full story but I understood that these young men had set out some days earlier by snowmobile to meet Scottie on the trail and help him with his heavy load. They had met on the southeast slope of Sugar Loaf Mountain, some 44 km from Baker Lake. They had built a small igloo and after taking some of Scottie's load, decided to have tea before heading out. This would give Scottie a chance to get ahead with his slower dog team. Scottie had expected them to overtake him, but they never did. He had just made it in before the storm and now he was very worried that something had gone wrong with the young brothers. Scottie had heard that I was heading out on the land in that general direction and wondered if I would mind looking for the boys. I gave him my assurances; he thanked me, and left the office.

That same morning Barnabus and I completed our preparations for the trip to Parker Lake and were soon rumbling across Baker Lake toward Sugar Loaf Mountain which we could see shimmering in the blinding sun. I was driving the Bombardier snowmobile, pulling a large bobsled loaded with six drums of fuel.

The trip across the lake was uneventful but very slow owing to the rock-hard ridges of snow drifted up by the recent storm. Luckily we were traveling southeast, more or less in accordance with the ridges. The wind which sculptured the snow came straight from the north giving the people of this land an unerring compass to follow in their wanderings.

Soon the flat truncated hill began to dominate the scenery as we drew near. Sugar Loaf rose 198 meters above the rolling tundra providing a valuable landmark when the air was clear. The surrounding slopes were gentle, and our route to Parker Lake took us along the east side. The sky was brilliant blue and the April sun reflected from the snow surface with painful radiance. Dark glasses were necessary at all times, for without them one would become snow blind in a very short time. This was the same route the brothers should have taken to Baker Lake, so we continually scanned the area as we traveled along.

As we skimmed along the relatively smooth eastern slope, I decided to swing further up the hill. We topped a small rise and there in the distance was a black speck contrasted against the shimmering snow.

'*Taikani!*' I yelled to Barnabus who was just replenishing the wad of snuff in his bottom lip.

He looked up.

'*Takuviuk?*' I asked. 'Do you see him?'

'*Ee-ma!*' was his reply as I stepped on the accelerator.

As we drew nearer we could make out the figure clearly. He was standing still and appeared to be gazing up the slope of the hill. As we continued to approach, the man suddenly whirled around and began to wave his arms frantically. Obviously he had finally heard the roar of the approaching Bombardier.

I stopped the snowmobile, and a very excited Michael Alerk climbed inside. One of the lost had been found. His speech was slurred as he alternated between English and Inuk-tit-tuut in his attempt to spill out his story.

'We got lost in the storm. I can't see. I don't know where Barney is; maybe frozen?'

All this fell from his lips in the first minute or two. 'I need some tea or I'll die.'

His words alerted me to the fact that Michael was badly dehydrated and on the point of collapse.

We immediately set about melting some snow for tea. As the Coleman stove hissed away, Michael spoke again more slowly. 'I was so thirsty I laid down and licked the ice like a dog.' He drank the water as soon as enough had melted and we added more snow.

'Is this Sugar Loaf Hill?' Michael asked. 'Our igloo must be around here someplace.'

We told him where we were and after he had finished off two pails of tea with plenty of sugar, he lay back on the seat. We let him rest for a while and then Barnabus began to speak to him in Inuk-tit-tuut. Finally he turned to me and said, 'He thinks igloo may be close by, maybe we find.'

And so we began a search for the igloo the two brothers had left with such tragic results. As I drove along, Michael continued to tell what had happened after old Scottie had left them. Things went well for a few miles, and then they began to have trouble with their snowmobile. The wind started to increase and the carburetor sucked in snow and soon froze. They tried cleaning it, but only went a short way before it froze again. By now the storm had intensified and they decided they could go no further. The place where they stopped was on the east slope of Sugar Loaf Mountain and Michael felt we were getting close to where they camped.

The boys could not find snow suitable for igloo building at the place where they stopped the snowmobile so they disconnected the komatik and pushed it down the slope until they found suitable snow. Soon they had a small igloo built and all their supplies moved inside. After they had tea, Barney suggested that they push the empty sled back up to where they

*Igloo where Scottie parted company with Michael Alerk and
Barney Sitowak.*

had left the snowmobile, load it on and bring it back to their igloo. They
would then be able to work on the carburetor in the comfort of their camp.
It sounded like a good idea, so according to Michael, that is what they
attempted.

They managed to find the snowmobile in the storm with some difficulty
and got it loaded on the komatik. This is when things began to go horribly
wrong. The first mistake they had made was to leave their snow knife
back in the igloo. They pointed the komatik down the slope in what they
thought was the direction of their igloo, but by now they could see nothing
in the blowing snow. They started to search frantically for their igloo but
couldn't find it in the storm. It was not difficult to imagine their
consternation when they failed to find their camp and realized that their
means of survival had been left there.

It did not take us very long to find the komatik and snowmobile in the
bright sunshine. It was facing down the hill, not more than three kilometers
southeast from where we had picked Michael up. We could see the
footprints, now elevated by the wind, moving in ever widening circles from
the snowmobile and sled. Michael could not see very well due to his partial
snow blindness but when we pointed to their igloo not more than 300
meters away from where they had left the sled his countenance darkened
and he began to mutter something to himself.

After we had all climbed back into the Bombardier, Michael said with much emotion, 'I think my brother is frozen!' He went on to say that after they had failed to find the igloo, Barney became very angry and said he was walking to Baker Lake. I could understand this because although the boys could not find their igloo, they were by no means lost. They knew that they were on the east slope of Sugar Loaf Hill and that from here it was 44 km northwest to the Baker Lake Settlement. The wind and snow ridges pointed the way. What was foolish, however, was to think that they were strong enough to walk that far straight into the teeth of the storm.

Michael related how he had tried to keep up with his brother. They walked until darkness fell and then pushed up snow with their hands to provide a little shelter for the night. At first light Barney started walking again. Michael soon fell behind and finally stopped. He stayed where he was until the storm started to abate. He could make out Sugar Loaf Hill as the weather cleared and the sun came out and not knowing what else to do, he began to walk slowly in that direction. Snow blindness developed as the day wore on. He was thirsty and weak and almost ready to lie down to sleep when he heard the motor of the Bombardier.

I set about establishing radio contact with the settlement so a search party could be organized for Barney. It was late afternoon and there appeared to be little hope of finding Barney so we decided to head back to Baker Lake. We would follow a route that perhaps would be close to the one the boys had taken and hope for the best. Michael was in an exhausted sleep in the back of the Bombardier as I turned the machine around and headed for home.

The next day dawned clear and bright. I had a search party ready the night before but we decided to wait until first light. We searched the area as well as the possible route Barney would have taken back to the settlement without results. When darkness fell, we were back in Baker Lake. At this point, no one expected to find Barney alive.

After two days of searching, Thomas Kakimut and his dog team found his body on the lake and I headed out to pick him up with the Bombardier.

I remember well what a sad task this proved to be. Barney was lying on the ice with his head pointed into the prevailing wind and directly toward the settlement that could be seen in the distance 19 km away. He had taken off his parka and placed it at his head. His shirtsleeves were rolled up and his bare arms were crossed over his chest. His feet were together and it looked as if he thought he was at home in his bed. Perhaps he did. Who knows what hallucinations come to a man as he faces death by freezing.

As I stood there looking down at Barney's peaceful face, I remarked to

Hugh Ungungai who was standing beside me. 'I guess he knew he couldn't make it so he just took off his parka to get it over with?'

'I don't think so,' Hugh replied. 'The old people have told me that you get hot before you die and take off your clothes.'

I thought about this for a while and it began to make sense. With only your body core left unfrozen, perhaps your brain would receive a signal of warmth when in fact you were minutes from death.

With sad hearts we lifted Barney's frozen body onto the sled and lashed it down. I thought how unforgiving this land is in winter. One young man was alive and for that everyone was thankful. Another paid for his mistake with his young life. For him death came softly on the wind.

CHAPTER TWENTY-FOUR

Meeting the Fox Man

Well the komatik is moving mighty slow
And I've still got a hundred miles to go.

Mush Along

I MET WAYNE SPELLER in late August of 1969 when he returned by canoe
from the Canadian Wildlife Service cabin on the northwest shore of
Aberdeen Lake. I had been away in the spring when he arrived to begin
a study of Arctic foxes and was unaware that he had spent the summer
there. It seemed that communication between wildlife agencies was almost
non-existent and I was determined to change that. We had time for a good
discussion before he flew south and I offered to store his canoe and
equipment until his return the following spring. Wayne appreciated my
offer of assistance and promised to keep me informed concerning his study.
He asked if I could collect some fox carcasses from the trappers over the
winter and I had agreed.

I received a letter from Wayne in mid April advising me that he would
be arriving with a student assistant on 15 May 1970. I met the plane and
picked them up. There was a large amount of equipment and supplies.
When everything was safely stored in the warehouse I invited them home
for supper.

Communication by radio or phone was very poor in Baker Lake and
we always welcomed someone fresh from southern climes well versed in
all the latest news. We sat around after supper listening to Wayne and
Brian Peg talk about the Vietnam War, student riots, latest box office
hits and any other new tidbits that came to mind. We sat and soaked it
up. Since it never really gets dark in late May we visited without regard
for time until Wayne and Brian could endure no more. Their heads began
to droop and with a surprised look at their watches, they excused themselves and left.

The next day Wayne and Brian began working on the fox carcasses I had collected over the winter. This study would be the basis for Wayne's Doctorate in Zoology. He had telemetric equipment for his final field study and expressed concern about transporting it safely to the cabin at Aberdeen Lake. If the equipment was mishandled it could be rendered useless and the season wasted.

Wayne had hired Inuit hunters the previous year to take him in and the trip had turned into an ordeal of survival. It was his first venture into the Arctic, which can be very cruel even in springtime. 'I have never been so cold in my whole life,' Wayne had told me. 'I tried sleeping on an air mattress and nearly froze to death.'

'That would be cold all right,' I said as seriously as I could. 'Couldn't you get any caribou skins?'

'The Inuit had skins, but I didn't have any,' Wayne said. 'I tell you when I finally got to that cabin I lit every candle and Coleman stove I had to warm myself up. I got it so hot in there the Inuit had to go outside but I didn't care. I've never been so cold!'

I could picture Thomas Kakimut trying to drink tea with the sweat pouring off his face and wondering what this crazy *Qallunnaaq* was trying to prove by lighting all the stoves.

'Experience is a good teacher,' I added philosophically. 'A little rough at times ... but good!'

Wayne and Brian continued their work. I stood by and watched for a while then finally spoke.

'You know, it's not too busy here just now. I'm pretty well caught up after being away on that snowmobile trip to Yellowknife, I could probably run you in with the Bombardier.'

Wayne stopped working and looked over.

'Are you serious? I would sure appreciate it if you could. I could get my equipment in without getting it broken.'

'Well,' I said, 'I would be asking for a favor in return. I'd like you to keep ten fox kits for me. I'm doing a little project on raising foxes in captivity and increasing the value of the pelts.' I paused then added, 'They do this on a large scale in Russia. I have a report on it.'

'Catching and keeping them won't be a problem,' Wayne said, 'but getting them back here will be.'

'I'll look after that,' I said quickly. 'I'll be stopping in late July with an aircraft checking the land camps.'

'That sounds okay to me.'

'Good,' I said. 'We'll discuss it more.'

The details were discussed and around noon on 19 May we began the long trip to Aberdeen Lake. The Bombardier was packed with equipment and supplies and we were pulling a sled behind with three 45-gallon drums of gas. It was a heavy load and I knew we would be breaking a trail through patches of soft deep snow.

I had tried to anticipate the routine breakages that I had become accustomed to and had all my tools and spare parts on hand. The first 14 km went fairly well because I was following an old track I had made a few weeks earlier when I had taken some school students out to learn how to set a fox trap as part of their cultural inclusion program. When I hit the end of the old trail it was real tough going. I had to shift down to low gear as the snow was soft along the small river valley I was following. The differential heated up as we plowed along and gave forth its usual stench of over-heated oil. I looked back at Wayne and Brian sitting in the small space allowed them in the back.

'It will get a bit better when we get on harder snow,' I yelled above the laboring engine. Wayne nodded in acknowledgment.

Wayne Speller had engaged Thomas Kakimut again as his Inuit guide for the summer. Thomas had set out earlier that day by snowmobile with his wife and children. His dogs followed behind. I wasn't surprised when after several hours we caught up to him.

He too was finding the trail tough going. He was over-loaded and his well-worn snow machine could barely manage the heavy komatik with his family sitting on top of the load. He was at a loss to know what to do and he finally reluctantly asked me if I could take some of his load.

'I don't know,' I replied in Inuk-tit-tuut. Thomas didn't speak English so I asked Barnabus Peryouar to elaborate.

'Tell him we're too heavy already,' I said.

After a discussion in Inuk-tit-tuut Barnabus replied, 'He plenty stuck now, maybe you take wife and kids, maybe he make it okay.'

I knew I was asking for trouble, but I agreed.

'Tell him to follow our trail in case we have trouble,' I said as I opened the back door of the Bombardier and waved his family in.

'There's no room,' Wayne protested, 'there isn't even enough room for us now.' He was obviously very upset but I ignored his protest.

'Do you want me to leave his wife and kids here? He needs all his stuff for the summer too. We can shift some boxes back to the sled. Once we reach the halfway point I can cache some fuel and things will be better.'

I started hauling out boxes and taking them back to the sled. Barnabus helped me cover them with a tarp and lash them down. A cold north wind had sprung up and by the time things were ready my hands were numb.

'Let's go,' I said and climbed behind the wheel.

Our route took us west of Baker Lake until we reached a good-sized lake with a long finger-like bay pointing northwest. We followed this to the end before striking off overland again in a westerly direction. Our route would take us to the deep bay on Aberdeen Lake that formed the southeast part of the lake.

While crossing overland we got into a boulder-field; soft snow on top, large rocks underneath. While trying to steer my way out I hit a rock with the left front ski turned and the steering arm on the ski broke. Now I could no longer control the direction of the ski.

'Bad luck,' I muttered. I had broken these before and always carried a spare but the spare I had was for the other side and they were not interchangeable. I got out, found the jack-all and started lifting the front end.

'What do we do now?' Wayne inquired in an exasperated voice.

'Fix it!' I replied curtly. It was obvious that Wayne knew little about a Bombardier snowmobile as he paced around the machine wondering what would happen next. I held the two pieces of the steering arm in my hands and tried to think. The arm was hollow; if I could drive a solid piece of metal in, it would hold together once the piece was bolted back on. I fished around in the toolbox until I found a cold chisel. 'This looks about the right size.' I hammered the cold chisel into the hollow steering arm. It was a nice snug fit. I bolted the arm back in place.

'There, almost as good as new,' I announced as I began to let the machine down with the jack-all.

'I think I'm beginning to see what it takes to be a Game Officer up here,' Wayne remarked.

'What's that,' I grinned. 'A jackass of all trades?'

Unfortunately the broken steering arm was only the beginning of a long list of mishaps that were to plague this trip. I would categorize it later as the worst trip I had ever taken in a Bombardier and I had covered great distances on the Arctic tundra in these machines.

The next breakdown a few kilometers further on was the hitch on my big bobsled. I repaired it with a short piece of chain and we kept going. The land we were traveling over was flat, white and featureless, but Barnabus seemed to know every protruding rock and tuft of grass and I followed his direction to the letter. He grabbed my arm. 'Maybe we stop!' he yelled and my foot hit the clutch as we slid to a stop. Barnabus reached for his snuffbox. His lower lip, I suspected, was permanently disfigured by the big wad of 'snuse' that was constantly in place there. I pointed to the snuffbox and delivered the standing joke that existed between us.

'Poison!' I said emphatically.

Barnabus grinned, 'No! Medicine!' We laughed. He put a fresh wad on top of the old one and said, 'Maybe we make cache here.' He emphasized his words with a downward chopping motion of his hand.

'Good; the sooner we get some weight off the better.'

I got out of the Bombardier and looked around. We seemed to be in the middle of a flat featureless plain. 'If we can't find our back-trail we'll never find this gas again,' I thought to myself as we moved toward the sled.

We unloaded two 45-gallon drums of gas and re-distributed our load.

'Things should go a little easier now,' I said to the others before we started off. How wrong I was.

We had just reached the ice on the southeast end of Aberdeen Lake when I heard the sickening sound of metal being ripped apart.

'What was that?' I shouted as I stepped on the clutch. We all jumped out for a look. I couldn't believe my eyes. The last wheel in the track on the driver's side had collapsed. It looked like someone with a giant old fashioned can-opener had cut around the hub of the metal wheel about 5 cm from the axle, both inside and out.

The axle was completely separated from the rest of the wheel except for a four centimeter wide rim of jagged metal.

'How do I get that mess off?' I said, exasperated. I did have two complete spare wheels and axle hubs, but how would I get what was left of the old axle off the spindle.

At least an hour passed as we tried to figure out how to keep the axle from turning while we put pressure on the stud nut. Finally we managed to attach a 'come-along' cable around it in such a way as to secure it while we reefed on the nut until it came loose.

It was late afternoon and everyone was tired and irritable. I started the Coleman stove. After we had some tea and a hot meal, things looked a bit brighter. Thomas Kakimut had caught up with us and joined us for the meal. As we sat around drinking our tea we could see in the distance three of Kakimut's dogs following his trail.

'A real good system,' I thought. 'If your snowmobile breaks down, you stop and have tea until your dogs catch up and you can go on.'

I thought that just about everything that could go wrong, had gone wrong and our trip to the west end of Aberdeen Lake would go well. The lake is approximately 75 km long so we still had some traveling ahead of us.

Soon we were underway once again. I drove as carefully as I could, trying to miss every hard snowdrift and keep an even speed. Things seemed to be going along nicely.

'Maybe not far now,' Barnabus said encouragingly. Within minutes, 'Bang! Thump, Thump.' We had broken our track. I didn't think it was possible to break that one inch thick heavy rubber belt, but broken it was and almost in sight of the Canadian Wildlife Service cabin. I made temporary repairs and struggled up to the cabin. I was completely exhausted but what a relief it was to deliver Wayne and his entourage to his study area. As the others began the process of unloading, I started digging in my spare parts box for the track repair link. I had carried it on every trip, never thinking I would ever need it. Now I was glad I had it along. In order to install it I had to somehow drill bolt holes through that thick rubber track. A tall order when you don't have a drill. I worked away for hours in the freezing wind cutting a hole through the thick track with the small blade of my pocketknife. I would need to cut four holes altogether. My fingers were soon numb and raw but I could not rest until that machine was repaired and ready to tackle the trail home.

I went in the cabin to warm up a little. Wayne was complaining about Kakimut's wife who had installed herself on the floor of the cabin with her children. The baby in her *amoutik* was crying and the other two children were running around.

'They were supposed to stay in their own place,' Wayne lamented.

I had no time for his trivial problems. I felt I had enough serious ones of my own.

'Kakimut will be here soon. Surely you can stand it til then,' I replied as I went out the door.

When I finally got the track mender installed, I climbed inside the Bombardier to rest. Barnabus joined me and we drank some tea.

'We sleep a little now,' I said, 'early tomorrow we go home.' Barnabus nodded his acknowledgment and reached for his bedroll.

The sun was already high in the sky when I awoke but the wind was from the north and it was very cold. It was early since the sun only dipped below the northern horizon for several hours in late May. I was anxious to be off. Anxious to see how many miles we would get behind us before trouble would strike again. I boiled a kettle and fried some canned bacon. It was my habit to camp inside the Bombardier. It was like a second home. Barnabus had slept in a tent Wayne and Brian had set up, hoping to entice Kakimut's family out of the cabin. I went to the cabin to tell Wayne we were shoving off.

Wayne was up when I went in.

'I didn't get a wink of sleep,' he complained. 'That woman and those kids coughed all night.'

I ignored his complaint.

'I'm leaving,' I said. 'I'm going to be doing camp patrols with an airplane sometime in July. I'll pick up the fox kits then. Try and get a message down to me if you want me to bring anything in. I'll see you then.'

We exchanged brief good-byes. He thanked me for everything and I went back outside. I fired up the Bombardier, dropped it in gear and headed down the trail, which I knew would eventually lead me home.

The bad luck that had plagued our outward journey continued unabated. Somewhere in the middle of the big lake 'white-out' conditions developed and the trail vanished. We stopped and lit the stove to make tea. The wind was picking up and we were engulfed in a thick snow squall.

'Just great,' I complained inwardly. 'We'll probably never see our back trail again, let alone our gas cache.' The wind screamed around the Bombardier as we sat in sultry silence nursing our tea.

'*Ajornamat.*' (It can't be helped)

'*Ajornamat,*' I repeated, trying to call on Inuit philosophy to lift my spirits. Barnabus grinned and nodded agreement. I pulled out my sleeping robe and wrapped it around my shoulders.

Once the weather allowed us to proceed further across the lake I began to smell exhaust fumes from the engine. I also felt sick and dizzy. I was very much aware of the danger of carbon monoxide in a Bombardier since the motor is enclosed in the rear of the machine, and regularly checked the exhaust pipes for cracks.

As I began to check for the source of the fumes my heart sank. The pipe had broken completely off just a few centimeters from the manifold. The exhaust on one side was being released directly into the engine compartment thereby leaking into the rest of the Bombardier. Because it was so close to the red-hot manifold, I didn't have anything that I could use to effect even a temporary repair.

'Very bad!' I said to Barnabus in Inuk-tit-tuut, pointing to the broken pipe. I grabbed a piece of rope and tied both front doors wide open, then I threw open the roof hatch. The freezing wind and snow whirled inside. How I longed for my caribou parka. I had left it behind in order to save space. Wasn't it, after all, almost the last week in May?

We traveled on with the barking of the unmuffled exhaust vibrating inside the cab. At least with all the fresh air blowing in the hatch and doors we didn't have to worry about gassing ourselves.

We finally left the lake and began crossing an area of tundra that was flat and bleak without a landmark to be seen. Our old trail had been lost back on the lake when another snow squall had overtaken us and we decided to push on into the swirling white void. I was hoping I would pick the tracks up again once we started to travel overland but the wind, as if to mock us, had risen in intensity and we could only see clearly a short distance ahead.

I began to watch the bouncing gas gauge. I had used the big exterior upper tank and had now switched to the smaller interior tank, which contained the last of the fuel. The needle swung back and forth as the

Bombardier negotiated the rough contours of the land, staying somewhere between empty and one quarter full.

I cast a quizzical glance in Barnabus' direction. He was staring intently into the swirling ground-drift. Periodically he would direct me a little to the left or right.

'How can he have any idea where we are in these conditions,' I reflected to myself, 'and how will we find those drums of gas in the middle of nowhere?' I glanced again at the gas gauge. 'Perhaps we should stop and wait until it clears before I run the tank dry.'

'*Ursug* (gas) maybe we find?' I shouted the question that had been on my mind for the last hour to Barnabus.

'Maybe,' was his laconic reply as he continued to stare through the windshield. The gauge was now reading empty and had very little bounce left. The light reflected off a disturbance in the snow off to the left. I swung toward it, then breathed a great sigh of relief; it was our old Bombardier trail. But what if we had already passed our gas cache? I put the thought out of my mind and began following the old trail. Finally the dark outline of two gas barrels emerged from the clouds of drifting snow. I thumped Barnabus on the back almost causing him to swallow his wad.

'Good man; good man.' I repeated. He said nothing, but his grin said everything that needed saying.

The black cloud that had hung over us had not gone away. We were still a good 50 km from Baker Lake when the track mender bolts pulled through the crude holes I had cut with my knife and once again we had a broken track. I repaired it with short pieces of cable stretched under the steel cross-links and we kept traveling. A few more miles and the track was loose again. More cable off the sled; more lashing of the track. On it went until we were only ten kilometers from home. The cable came loose and every turn of the track whipped the loose cable against the back of the Bombardier. It beat off the rear tail-light and a patch of paint.

At this stage I was so cold from the north wind that blew directly on me and so frustrated that I decided as long as the tracks turned I would keep going. Barnabus had pulled a caribou skin across our knees to help break the wind. 'Wump, wump, wump,' the cable whipped against the back end. Finally the settlement was in sight.

'We can walk now if we have to,' I thought, but then realized: 'I'm too cold, I'd freeze to death for sure.'

I dropped the sled on the lake then roared up to the garage door. Barnabus ran to open it. I took one last look at the beat up machine and headed for home.

I didn't see Roy, the chief mechanic, for 24 hours. When I did drop into the garage, the Bombardier was already repaired. Roy said in a grave voice, 'You must have had a real rough time out there?'

I opened my mouth to begin my tale, then closed it again. 'It wasn't the best trip I ever had,' I said evenly as I turned to leave.

CHAPTER TWENTY-FIVE

To Alaska on a Playcat

Listen to the sound of the wind my friend
Tomorrow we'll have to get going.

Only The Wind

THE NORTH SEEMS TO ATTRACT a real variety of people seeking adventure. Before we left on our Centennial snowmobile trip to Yellowknife we received word that a snowmobile expedition traveling from Quebec to Alaska was in Churchill and was anxious to join our group. Of course no one was in favor of this and we concluded we would be long departed on our journey before they ever arrived in Baker Lake. This proved to be the case.

During the first part of May 1970, a rumour began circulating around the village that one man was continuing the expedition along the west coast of Hudson Bay visiting the settlements and planned to come to Baker Lake. We had already completed our trip to Yellowknife and arrived back home on 30 April.

Around the middle of May a strange looking outfit approached from the east following the north shore of the lake. A man was driving a rubber-tracked all-terrain vehicle and pulling two sleds in tandem behind. Everyone went down to meet the new visitor and see his unusual machine. It was called a Playcat. The rubber tracks looked a bit like a Caterpillar tractor, hence, perhaps, the name. No one had seen one before. Judging by the load on his two sleds, it appeared quite powerful considering the size.

The driver identified himself as Guy Chevalier. Apparently he had started out from somewhere in Quebec on a conventional snowmobile. We learned that two others had started with him but eventually dropped out as the trip progressed. Somewhere around James Bay they got caught in a blizzard. One of the party suffered severe frost-bite and was hospitalized. His other partner gave up soon after. One had to admire his tenacity. He had persevered and finally made it to Baker Lake. In Churchill he had

All-terrain vehicle Playcat leaving Baker Lake.

found another sponsor, the Playcat Company, which had provided his present machine. Guy found a place to stay and began to repair his equipment.

A few days after I returned from the stressful Bombardier trip to Aberdeen Lake with Wayne Speller and his group, Guy came to my office. He said he was looking for more maps but I soon learned he was also searching for information and advice. He told me he was planning to push on and wondered what conditions were like further inland. I told him quite bluntly that the season was too far advanced and he didn't have a hope in hell of making it across the barrens to Yellowknife.

He seemed to be making his plans as he went along. He went to my large wall map and traced a route northwest to Pelly Lake and on toward Bathurst Inlet.

'The snow should be better if I go north,' he explained. 'I should be able to make it.'

Since our successful trip to Yellowknife and my recent trip to Aberdeen Lake I probably came across as a little cocky. I didn't mean to be, but it was apparent he wouldn't listen because nothing I said seemed to faze him.

'You won't make it.' I summed it up. 'The snow on the big lakes will be melting and the little rivers will be flowing any day now. You just won't make it! You should plan for next year.' Guy Chevalier was undeterred. Nothing I said had any effect on his plans. Finally as he turned to leave I made one last plea.

'Look, I can see you're going to go regardless of anything I say. Okay, go ahead; but at least follow my Bombardier trail to Aberdeen Lake.' I paused for a moment and went to the map. 'My trail is here,' I traced with my finger. 'And it goes to a cabin at the narrows on the west end of Aberdeen Lake.' I stuck a pin at the cabin location.

'If you get into trouble; and I know you will, at least try to get to that cabin before break up. I will be stopping there in July with a plane. There are two biologists there and they can help you.' He had followed my discourse attentively and thanked me for my help.

'I'm leaving right away,' he said and he went out the door.

'He'll never make it; he won't make fifty kilometers,' I muttered to myself as I dialed my home phone. Iris answered … 'Hi dear,' I said. 'Look; grab my camera and bring it down to the office, would you please?'

'What's happening,' she queried.

'That crazy Frenchman is leaving for Aberdeen Lake. I want to get a picture because I don't think we'll be seeing him again.'

The fact is, I did see him again, in the middle of July, when Pooch Lisenfeld taxied his Grumman Goose in to shore at the cabin on Aberdeen Lake. Guy Chevalier was waiting on the rocks to help us land.

After I had listened to Wayne's description of this fellow who suddenly appeared out of nowhere and had since been a significant interruption to his biological studies, I tried to change the subject by saying, 'We have to keep going, we're behind schedule. Wayne, think of it this way; you probably saved this fellow's life.'

We finished loading the white fox pups on the aircraft and I yelled at Chevalier to come aboard.

Later back in Baker Lake I learned more details of his ordeal. Warm weather had caught up to him the same day he left Baker Lake. The snow on top of the ice began to melt rapidly and the slush started to pile up in front of his sleds until he was unable to pull them. Guy told me how he had shoveled slush for over 2 kilometers in order to make a road on the lake on which he could travel. He related how he had struggled for half a day to get his outfit across a little river. He stopped to have tea on the other side and while he was sitting there a flood of water several feet deep came downstream, making it impossible to go back. Finally in desperation he made a pack for his back with as much food as he could carry and set off following the Bombardier trail across the lake to the cabin.

He was exhausted and at the point of collapse when he was spotted out on the ice and Kakimut went out to help him. I looked at his thin haggard features. There wasn't a lot of extra food at the camp and he had spent a rough two months. I knew what he had been through and felt a twinge of compassion.

'What will you do now?' I finally asked when he had finished his story.

'I'm going to stay here for the summer. Maybe try and get a job.' He paused, then continued, 'I want to start my trip again, next fall.'

'Well, I guess I'll be seeing you around then,' I concluded as we parted.

Guy did get a casual job for the summer and sometime in late August he took a Transair flight south. No one in Baker Lake really thought he would come back but he did; just after freeze up. He seemed determined to pick up where he had left off. He stocked up on supplies and hired John Tapatai, one of the Inuit mechanics from the government garage, to take him out to where he had left his outfit.

It was the middle of November and we were waiting for our first big storm of the winter. It came about a day or so after John had left with the intrepid adventurer. It blew for three solid days and nights. The temperature stayed around minus 35°C, and the wind-chill was extreme. I knew the men would be having a tough time of it out on the land.

Late in the second day after the storm had abated, John and Guy arrived back in the settlement. The plane came in the next day and Guy Chevalier left Baker Lake on it. A howling blizzard had finally broken his resolve. Actually, there was more to it than just that. I got the details from John when I stopped at the garage for coffee. Apparently they found the Playcat and other stuff but it had been cached in a bad place. The water from the little stream had backed up during freeze-up that fall and froze the equipment in a foot of ice. They had just started to try chiseling it out when the storm struck. When it was over, that was it; Guy sold everything to John for a hundred bucks and a return trip to Baker Lake.

I wound up hauling most of the stuff John had purchased back from Aberdeen Lake with my Bombardier and sled. I was returning empty after hauling supplies to the CWS cabin for a caribou tagging project. John had asked me before I left if I would mind picking it up for him. Thus ended another adventure with the dashed hopes and dreams of the originator.

The Arctic in winter is a stern school-master and one better be ready to accept the lessons it teaches.

CHAPTER TWENTY-SIX

June on the Barren-lands

In the distance the cry of the falcon
Overhead, a great rushing of wings
The wind in the valley is calling to me
And the voice of eternity rings.

Eons Of Time

THE YEAR 1970 REMAINS memorable for many reasons. When I
reviewed the amount of time I was away from home on trips, I was
shocked to learn that it totaled almost six months. When Frank Bailey
contacted me on 22 May and said I should be in Churchill the following
Friday to participate in a Caribou Calf Mortality study being conducted
by the Canadian Wildlife Service, Iris and I decided that we needed to
talk. I wanted to be home more, to enjoy our little son together, but on
the other hand I wanted to be involved in things happening in the Baker
Lake area. After all, it would fall to me to explain things to the people
when questions were raised concerning biologists and their studies. Prior
to my arrival very little, if any, discussion or explanation took place
concerning wildlife studies. They were simply *tuktuluree*, the men who
looked after the caribou. I had been tagged with the same name. I felt it
was time to get the hunters and trappers more involved or at least be
aware of what was going on in their traditional lands.

Iris and I reached a compromise. She and Kevin would accompany me
to Churchill. After several days there she would continue on to visit her
parents in Saskatchewan. After participating in the caribou study, I would
take annual leave early in July and join them.

Friday, 29 May, we were on a Transair DC3 bouncing through a weather
front with rain and poor visibility into the Churchill airport. Three days
later I was headed north again in a Cessna 180 aircraft piloted by Tom
Rutherford, with CWS biologist Chuck Dauphiné. We were heading for
Calf Lake, an area near the centre of the calving ground, approximately
170 km southeast of Baker Lake.

Author on Kaminuriak caribou calving area.

We flew up the west coast of Hudson Bay and near Eskimo Point we encountered low cloud and fog. Tom decided to climb on top and do an instrument approach to Rankin Inlet. This all seemed quite impressive until we broke out of the overcast with Rankin Inlet nowhere in sight. We stayed below the cloud and rode the beacon into Rankin while Tom discussed in great detail the reason that we were not at the end of the runway when we descended from the clouds. We fueled the aircraft and continued Visual Flight Rules to Calf Lake. The rest of the day was spent setting up the camp. As the land of the long days dimmed somewhat around midnight, we had one last cup of tea. Overhead skeins of Canada geese flew low. Horned larks flew across tundra that had only recently emerged from the enduring snows of winter. It was good to be on the land in June.

The next forenoon was spent working on the camp but in the afternoon we went flying in the Cessna 180 looking for caribou. The relentless northward migration was nearing a merciful end for many of the female caribou. How many lakes, how many streams, how many hundreds of kilometers had they covered after leaving the boreal forest to attain this barren, rocky, wind-swept plain where within days many thousands of the pregnant females would drop their little brown calves on the damp, still-frozen ground?

We covered the areas around Kaminak, Kaminuriak and Banks Lakes. Pregnant females had arrived in significant numbers.

The weather turned unusually vicious for the next five days. It began with gusty winds, low cloud and fog on 3 June. On 6 June it developed into a major windstorm with wind gusts in excess of 140 kph.

We had set up two big 3 meters x 3 meters canvas tents that had a snap-together aluminum framework on the inside. A DC3 on wheel/ski had made several trips to get all the material in for the camp. Lumber had been brought in and each tent had a wooden floor. As the winds increased in intensity we added more rock to the base of the canvas exterior trying to ensure that it would stay anchored to the ground. Luckily we had situated the tents just below a high esker which continued for some distance northwest of the camp. It helped to deflect the full intensity of the storm.

There was nothing to do but wait out the wind. It howled incessantly. Each blast struck the huge tent causing it to shift back and forth. The metal framework creaked and clanked. There were six men in the camp when the storm began. The strong wind and sleet made it virtually impossible to do anything. The winds peaked on Saturday, 6 June. One of the biologists had a hand-held anemometer and struggled to the top of the ridge for a reading. It was calibrated to 80 mph (128 kph) and when held up into the wind the cups began to whirl and the needle held tight to the maximum reading.

By Saturday evening everyone was getting pretty edgy. Most of the time was spent in our bedrolls on the newly built wood floor. It was impossible to sleep. The howling, creaking and clanging started to get to our pilot Tom Rutherford. He apparently wasn't used to going for long periods without talking to someone. He got up from his bedroll finally and began pacing around in the small space at our feet.

'This tent's going to go!' he shouted. 'This tent can't take much more of this.' He paced around and said again, 'This tent's going to go!' No one answered him and this seemed to upset him even more.

'When do you think the wind's going to let up?' He almost pleaded for someone to engage him in conversation. 'It's been four days now,' he said. 'How long do these storms last anyway?' Everyone continued to lie silent in their bedrolls. He continued pacing. 'This tent could go any minute!' he yelled as a fresh blast of wind set the canvas and framework shuttering. Finally Frank Miller, the Project Biologist, couldn't stand Tom's antics any longer. He sat up and growled at Tom.

'Look, you're probably right. This tent could disintegrate at any moment and if it does one of those steel bars will probably wrap itself around your neck and take you with it. You'd be better off lying down on the floor instead of pacing around up there.' Having said this Frank returned to his place on the floor.

Tom cast a glance at the quivering steel bars that snapped together to form the tent-frame. Another blast of air shook the tent.

'I guess you're right,' he admitted. 'I could be killed up here if the tent goes.' He crawled back into his bedroll and we continued in relative peace to listen to the raging storm buffeting the tent.

On the morning of 7 June the wind had decreased somewhat, but was still blowing steadily from the north at 90 kph with peak gusts in excess of this. The camp had survived fairly well; the tents were intact and damage was minimal. Our attention shifted to the Cessna 180 aircraft sitting out on the ice. As the storm was developing we had lashed two full 45-gallon drums of aviation fuel to each of the wheel/skis and to the tail ski. The plane was facing into the wind and there was little chance of a wind shift, so we had felt fairly confident when we left the aircraft three days earlier. Through lulls in the blowing snow we could now catch a glimpse of the plane. It was not exactly where we left it. The wind had blown it back about a hundred meters over the ice. Perhaps it would have gone much further except for a large melting snowdrift into which the tail and the fuel drums had become lodged. As the storm increased, the temperature dropped and the aircraft was frozen into the snowdrift.

Tom the pilot was anxious to get out to the plane for a closer inspection. From the shelter of the tent it looked fine.

'I've got to get out there,' he emphasized. 'There could be structural damage we can't see from here.' Everyone advised him to stay put but he continued to pursue the issue. Finally, sensing the irritation this discussion was having, Dave the cook agreed to go with Tom to inspect the aircraft.

'Don't be fools,' Frank advised. 'What advantage will it be to know if the plane's damaged now, or later when the wind goes down?'

Ignoring all advice, Tom and Dave set off. They gained the edge of the ice. A large section between the shore and the plane had frozen as smooth as glass. The boys were traveling downwind and when they stepped to the glassy surface with their backs to the wind, they were blown along by the wind. Legs spread-eagled, arms out, the wind pushed them over the ice surface. One would lose his balance and fall, then get up and continue the fun. It was obvious they were enjoying it. We watched and laughed at their antics from the front of the tent.

'Wait until they decide to come back!' someone quipped.

Indeed the trip ashore was an entirely different matter. Unable to gain any foothold on the glare ice, they tried crawling on their hands and knees. After many minutes they gained only a few meters. Dave finally took a different tack and retreated to the frozen drift at the tail of the plane. He followed it as far as he could toward the shore then using his belt knife crawled across several patches of glare ice. Using the rough patches of ice and snowdrifts he took a circuitous route to the shore. Tom eventually had to give up his direct route and followed him.

For the rest of the camp this was a welcome diversion to the boredom of the last several days. We stood around like spectators at a football game, laughing at each fall to the ice, cheering and heckling until the brave adventurers were again in our midst. Dave laughed it off; Tom being more sensitive wanted to know why we hadn't come to their assistance?

It was early afternoon on 8 June before the weather was fit to fly again. The wind still blew briskly from the north and the temperature was below freezing.

The Cessna was checked carefully and after a rather rough take-off run, we were airborne and headed for Baker Lake. It was only after we reached the settlement that we learned the magnitude of the damage wreaked by the storm. Over twenty canoes had been damaged or blown away across the lake. It was normal practice to leave canoes out on the lake for the winter. They are secured to a steel pipe frozen into the ice. This prevents them from being lost under huge snowdrifts that blanket the village each winter. A canoe left under a huge drift was usually a write-off. Due to the weight of the melting snow the ribs would be crushed.

The misfortune here occurred because most of the canoes were no longer secured out on the ice. Some were being used to get back and forth from the shore which now had an ever-expanding strip of open water between the north shore and the ice which was still suitable for snowmobile travel. The canoe would be lashed on the komatik, the camping and hunting gear placed inside and off they would go to the other side of the lake where once again the canoe would be employed to get ashore.

The loss of so many canoes was a severe economic blow to the community. The cost of a new one was extremely high because they had to be brought in from the south on sealift.

We learned that the air radio observers had clocked the wind at peak gusts of 160 kph. Parts of the roof of the Nursing Station in Rankin Inlet had been blown off. It seemed none of the settlements had escaped unscathed. I saw parts of canoes in the snow near Tanatuluk Islands on a return trip to the caribou camp; more than 48 km across the lake.

I had previously requested that at least two Inuit hunters from Baker Lake be involved as observers at the caribou camp. Frank Miller had readily agreed. He understood, as I did, that if future scientific studies were to be successful, the people directly dependent on the wildlife had to be informed and involved.

A Hiller helicopter assigned to the study arrived from the south and was sent in to Baker Lake to pick up Luke Tungwak and Barnabus

Peryouar. In the sunny days to follow we would spend several days in the center of the calving area making observations and picking up dead calves for autopsy. A radiant June sun beamed down on exposed vegetation, sending heat waves dancing across the landscape. Observations through spotting scopes and binoculars became difficult but who could fret over such trivia? The great silent land was now awakening to the call of Lapland longspurs and horned larks. The brassy call of the male ptarmigan could be heard as he viewed his domain from a high boulder. Flying overhead in the aircraft these tiny specks of white could be seen almost in a grid pattern as each defended his territory from the highest promontory he could find.

Some non-breeding tundra wolves were active in the calving ground and many of the little brown calves found life very brutal and short. The wolf killed the calf by grasping the neck just behind the head and giving it a shake. Only the tender internal organs were consumed and the rest left for scavengers. It was the impact of this activity during calving that Frank and his team were trying to assess. One of the wolves was collected for autopsy. Eric Broughton, a Veterinarian Pathologist with CWS in Ottawa, was part of the group and he was kept busy.

On 10 June I assisted Chuck with a stratified random block survey of the calving ground from which a population estimate could be calculated and when this work was completed, I returned to Baker Lake. I continued to provide logistical support until the fieldwork was concluded.

CHAPTER TWENTY-SEVEN

Tuktu-wak

Well my parka feels like ice
Don't make me tell you twice
Mush along my huskies take me home.

Mush Along

W E WERE STRUGGLING with the darkness and cold of late November 1969 when some hunters came in with reports of a strange animal sighting along the Kazan River south of Baker Lake. They had a name for it in Inuk-tit-tuut passed down by their forefathers who would have occasionally seen them further south around the old abandoned settlement of Padlei. They called it *tuktu-wak*, literally translated, 'a caribou with a beard'. It was in fact a moose who apparently wandered north of the tree line following the browsing along the Kazan River.

I was aware that moose were common much further north than this at the mouth of the Anderson River and in the Mackenzie Delta; but that was a much different climate. Baker Lake, near the geographical center of Canada, had one of the most severe climates anywhere in the Arctic. I knew that a moose would have a tough time surviving the winter here. The winter of 1970 proved to be one with the most storms and the coldest in many years. The minimum average temperature for January, February and March was a frigid minus 44° Celsius. The average number of days the wind speed exceeded 63 kph during this period was 11, exceeding 52 kph totaled 15, and the number of days the wind exceeded 40 kph was 22. When the wind chill values were calculated for these temperatures, it was not difficult to see that a moose would have a very tough time surviving on the open tundra.

I made several excursions to the area where the moose was first sighted in November and December but was unable to locate it.

Early in May a hunter located the frozen carcass and I went out with the Bombardier and sled to pick it up. It was on the west bank of the Kazan River about 20 kilometers from the south shore of Baker Lake. It had bedded down with its back to the prevailing north wind. The head was tucked in next to the body in the manner a dog curls up to sleep. We loaded it on the sled with much difficulty and I hauled it back to the settlement.

It was late in the evening when we finally got home. I had taken Iris along; the first trip out on the land since the boat trip to Chesterfield Inlet, and we had stopped at the cabins at the mouth of Kazan River for a mug-up. I was conversing with Barnabus in what I term 'simple English', due to the fact that he possessed a limited vocabulary. I knew most of the words he understood in English, he knew the words I understood in Inuk-tit-tuut and so we got along fine. I must admit though it might sound funny to someone listening to us. As we pulled up to the cabins I said to Barnabus, 'Maybe we stop now, make tea?' He nodded acknowledgment.

I continued, 'I find grub-box, maybe you chop ice.' Again he nodded and got out of the Bombardier. In the back I could hear Iris laughing, obviously at me.

'What's so funny?' I asked testily.

'Oh, I'm sorry,' she said. 'But to hear you two talk – it sounds just like Hawkeye and Chingishcook from the old western movies.'

I understood what she meant but it still annoyed me.

'Do you think if I talked like a university professor he would understand me better?' I retorted as I pulled the grub box out for tea. Iris stifled her giggles and headed for the cabin.

Author and Barnabus making observations on caribou calving grounds.

I parked the Bombardier in front of our house, with the sled still attached. The moose looked like he was sleeping on the sled. It wasn't long before people began to come by for a look. Word got around because after church let out the next day the sled was surrounded by curious onlookers. For most of the people it would be the first and last *tuktu-wak* they would ever see.

When I was in the Caribou Calf Mortality Study camp I discussed the moose with Frank Miller and Eric Broughton of the Canadian Wildlife Service. They seemed interested in investigating the matter further. I had the moose thawed and Eric performed a necropsy. It was a textbook case of starvation, but there were some interesting aspects. The moose had fractured his top and bottom incisors in his attempts to forage for sedges which are not normally part of the winter diet. He had fought a valiant fight but the harsh environment proved to be too much. The occurrence of the moose on the tundra was attributed to the 'pioneering' instinct in the species. A paper on the incident was published in the *Journal of Wildlife Diseases* in January 1972.

CHAPTER TWENTY-EIGHT

Scottie's Stories

I hear the sounds of the people
The tooniks who lived in this land
I see the stone walls of their dwellings
Built up by mysterious hands.

Eons Of Time

I FIRST MET SCOTTIE TOOLOOLEE at a Hunters and Trappers meeting I
had called in Baker Lake. My attention was drawn to him because it
was obvious that he was deaf and yet this fact in no way hindered his
rather aggressive participation in the meeting. He had opinions and he
expressed them forcefully. I regarded him with some amazement as I
became aware that he could read lips; not in English but in Inuk-tit-tuut.
It was just a bit comical at first. Hugh Ungungai would interpret the bits
and pieces Scottie was unable to pick up on his own. What made it amusing,
until I became accustomed to the practice, was the way in which Hugh
would form the Inuk-tit-tuut words with his lips without actually saying
them out loud. He would, of necessity, exaggerate the movement of his
lips for the purpose of clarity. Scottie would watch his lip movements
intently, repeating the words Hugh was expounding. On occasion Hugh
would correct him and repeat the word.

I was very glad that it was possible to communicate with Scottie, for I
found him to be a knowledgeable and interesting person. It was apparent
that his contact with the *Qallunaaq* had been extensive. Hugh told me
Scottie's father had been a Scottish trader, hence the name 'Scottie', which
everyone called him.

Scottie knew how to obtain maximum benefit from whatever was
available, regardless of whether it was from the wildlife resources, the
tuktuluree or other hunters. He filled a leadership role without hesitation.
Because Hugh was willing to translate for Scottie, I began to learn more
about him, and so the long Arctic nights we spent together in the camps
were often filled with story telling.

Building igloo, Inuit caribou hunters.

The first story I remember hearing from Scottie was humorous and because of his habit of articulating his dialogue with pantomime, it barely needed much translation. Hugh's good-natured descriptions completed the details of the story.

This particular story was about his life as a young man living in a winter igloo village somewhere on the land between Tavani and Padlei. Both posts have long since been abandoned. Tavani was on the coast and Padlei, 190 km inland.

His story began with a sketch Scottie made on a page of my notebook. It was the outline of a typical family igloo arrangement.

The first porch was entered through a long passageway. This was where the snow was beaten off your *kulituuk* or outer parka. Then one would enter a large circular common area; from this, tunnels branched off to the various family igloos. In this particular case there were three igloos connected to the common area or inner porch. The entrance to Scottie's igloo was about a meter away from his uncle's entrance. There was also an entrance to another family member's igloo.

Once Scottie had described the floor-plan from his sketch, he continued with the story. He had been visiting in the igloo farthest from his own and his uncle's, until very late at night. Everyone became sleepy and crawled under the caribou sleeping-robes. Scottie left to return to his own igloo. He went through the common area and crawled through the igloo

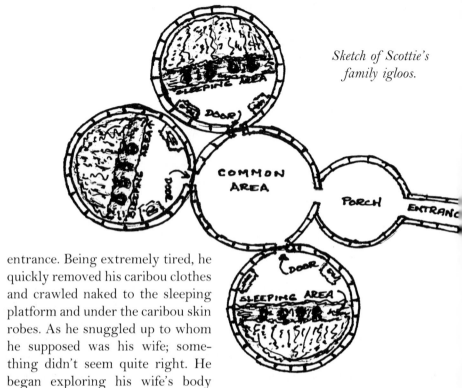

Sketch of Scottie's family igloos.

entrance. Being extremely tired, he quickly removed his caribou clothes and crawled naked to the sleeping platform and under the caribou skin robes. As he snuggled up to whom he supposed was his wife; something didn't seem quite right. He began exploring his wife's body with his hands. Scottie's hands began to describe his search on his own body. From this point on little translation was required and it was difficult to keep from laughing. Scottie's hands explored his face, then, somewhat mystified, moved down the neck to the torso and now with increased wonder, lower to his belly. All the while he described his amazement in rapid Inuk-tit-tuut. Finally his hand moved hesitantly lower. By now everyone listening exploded in laughter.

'It's a man!' he exclaimed and horrified he jumped out from under the sleeping robes and began searching in the dark igloo for his caribou clothing. As he hurriedly left the igloo embarrassed, he heard his aunt and uncle talking and laughing softly to themselves. In the blackness of the large snow porch he had mistakenly gone into his uncle's igloo instead of his own.

Scottie related another interesting incident in his life one frigid evening as we sat in camp near the Kazan River listening to the incessant howling of the wind. As before, Hugh translated as Scottie told this story.

They had been hunting caribou unsuccessfully southwest of Baker Lake, near a big lake, possibly Tebesjuak. There was a party of four hunters including Scottie. They had been without food for several days and were ravenous. Laboriously they chiseled a hole through two meters of ice and began to jig for fish. Luckily they managed to catch a very large lake trout, probably in excess of 14 kilograms. It was very fat and the hunters devoured the fish in short order. Everyone ate all they could and then being very tired they erected a small snow house barely big enough for all four to sleep in. The occupants were lying close together and Scottie was near the middle.

Before daybreak, Scottie awoke with pains in his stomach. The large quantities of rich, oily fish was at odds with his previously empty stomach. He realized that he had to defecate without delay. He got up and grabbed the snow knife. His intention was to make an opening in the wall of the igloo and project his posterior through it because all the floor space inside was occupied with sleeping Inuks.

He had barely begun his work with the snow knife when the exertion triggered an involuntary bowel movement. Unfortunately for Scottie, he was standing near the sleeping face of one of his companions.

Once again Scottie's pantomime took over, as I doubled over in laughter. No need of a translation here, as Scottie cupped his fingers and scooped out his eye sockets one at a time, flinging his hand downward toward the snow as he continued to relate the incident without interruption.

When Hugh had composed himself somewhat, he translated the seriousness of the occurrence. Had this been an intentional act, it would have been the most serious insult perpetrated on any individual in perhaps any culture but especially Inuit culture. When the hunter had finished clearing his vision he lunged for the snow knife fully intending to run it through Scottie's body. There was a scuffle in the tight confinement of the little igloo and this very nearly was the result. It was only Scottie's vehement protestations and the intervention of one of the other hunters which prevented a homicide.

Scottie abruptly ended the story at this point and I was left to speculate on the aftermath of the incident. Hugh had ended his translations by announcing that this particular hunter wouldn't have anything to do with Scottie from that time onward. 'Small wonder,' I thought, as I pondered what I might have done under similar circumstances.

It was on that first organized caribou hunt at Schultz Lake that I began to sense animosity between the people of Scottie's clan and the Back River people. His clan had lived on the land around Padlei while many other clans came from north of Baker Lake, around Garry Lake and ranging along the Back River. Following the starvation years of 1956–57, the Canadian Government moved everyone into settlements with little or no consultation with the Inuit affected. Now they were expected to get along as one big happy family, despite age-old differences.

I began to see the challenge I faced on the hunt when Scottie went into an igloo close to the cabin to rouse out some Garry Lake hunters who were still sleeping. They actually came to blows when the confrontation re-erupted outside the igloo. I realized right then that I had better not start showing favoritism to one group over the other.

Scottie told me a story about his personal encounter with a tundra wolf which I found very interesting.

He was hunting with his adopted son Nookik in the area around Parker Lake. They managed to find a small herd of caribou and shot several. One large bull was wounded and ran away. Scottie and Nookik were traveling by dog team and began following the blood trail of the wounded caribou. As they went along, they began to approach a low hill and noticed that the caribou trail led around one side of it. Scottie, anticipating that the caribou could be on the opposite side of the rocky hill, jumped off the komatik. He told Nookik to keep on the track and he would go around the other side of the hill in the hope that he could spot the animal.

The dog-team continued on as Scottie rounded the side of the hill. There in front of him was the wounded caribou facing down a tundra wolf in the process of trying to bring the animal down.

Scottie's sudden arrival on the scene had a dramatic effect. The wolf discontinued his attack on the wounded caribou and ran straight toward Scottie. When Scottie jumped off the komatik he hadn't taken his rifle or any other weapon with him. Now he was facing an angry wolf defenseless.

I was fully into the story by this time and took a deep breath as Scottie paused to give Hugh a chance to catch up with the translation. He pushed some Copenhagen under his tongue before he continued.

The wolf stopped a few meters in front of Scottie, crouching low to the snow as if to spring forward. Scottie was petrified but realized his only chance was to continue to face the animal as he slowly began to back away. The wolf moved forward still in a crouched position. Scottie said he had no doubt as to the wolf's intention and he waited for the attack to come. As he looked beyond the wolf he noticed Nookik and the dog-team had completed the circuit of the hill and were approaching the scene. This gave him needed courage and he began to scream to Nookik that a wolf was attacking him. The dogs caught the scent and began to bark. This development, Scottie was sure, saved his life because the wolf heard the dog team and spun around, taking off toward them. Scottie continued to scream at Nookik to get the rifle. Finally he saw the wolf approaching and quickly pulled the rifle out. His shot dropped the wolf a short distance in front of his dogs.

Being very familiar with all the assurances given by wildlife experts and naturalists that there is no record of wolves attacking a human, I pressed Hugh for more details.

'Ask Scottie if the wolf was sick, you know, with rabies; was that why he came after him?' Hugh patiently translated for me.

'*Akaa, akaa*,' Scottie replied in the negative.

'Does he think the wolf would have killed him if Nookik hadn't shown up?'

Hugh silently formed the Inuk-tit-tuut words with his lips.

'*Ii-ma, ii-ma*,' Scottie replied.

'For sure he would have,' Hugh replied.

Scottie went on for some time, then Hugh concluded the story.

'Scottie says he was pretty scared after that and he went to the RCMP to see if he could get one of those little guns.'

'You mean a pistol?' I interjected.

'Ya, that's it,' Hugh continued. 'Scottie wanted to have that gun with him all the time in case something like this happened again.'

I found this story quite intriguing and determined in my mind that I wouldn't take any chances with wild animals regardless of what the so-called experts had to say on the subject. If Scottie had been alone, the wolf would have probably killed him and the experts still wouldn't have had any 'recorded' wolf kill of a human.

Many years later three tundra wolves would follow me on the caribou calving ground near Dewar Lakes on Baffin Island when I had left my rifle in the helicopter. Perhaps they were just curious, but as I walked briskly toward the machine with the wolves following a short distance behind, the story Scottie told me that night in our camp on the Kazan River flashed through my mind.

I was conducting a survey of the Kaminuriak caribou herd in 1972. While on reconnaissance flights I passed close to Scottie's camp at the narrows south of Parker Lake and decided to stop for a visit. It was the last part of May and the ice surface was smooth. As the Cessna 185 slid to a stop, Scottie and Nookik came down from the cabin to greet us.

I realized immediately that this would be an interesting visit because I had no one to interpret for me. I would have to rely solely on my very limited understanding of Inuk-tit-tuut. After the initial greetings were out of the way, I asked, holding out my map, '*Nami tuktu kakpaa?*' (where are the caribou?) I was surprised and pleased when Scottie read my lips and began to trace with his finger on the map where he had seen caribou recently. I was very thankful for the information because it would save us flying time trying to locate them on our own.

When I folded up the map and prepared to leave, Scottie began talking about something which I could not understand clearly. He was asking if I wanted to see something and then I caught the Inuk-tit-tuut word for airplane (*timmisuut*). I thought he was talking about the plane I had just arrived in but he was pointing toward his cabin and asking if I wanted to see the airplane. Finally, thinking I was misunderstanding him, I said in frustration: '*Takulagu*' (let me see it.) Scottie and Nookik took off for the cabin with the pilot and myself following. As we rounded the south side of the cabin we saw the fuselage of a new Cessna 172. It was blue and white and carried American registration. Scottie had thoughtfully covered the instrument panel with a piece of canvas as the windscreen was missing.

'Where in hell did this come from?' the pilot asked.

As we stood looking at what was left of a beautiful new airplane, the incident of the previous summer came to mind. Some American tourists had flown north in a new Cessna 172 on floats. They had been in Baker Lake for a day or two before they headed south. I remembered seeing the sleek little craft moored down on the Hudson's Bay Company beach. They had flown south and the word went around the village that they had tipped the plane over while fishing on some lake. There was a lot of mining exploration going on that summer and as the poor misfortunates clung to the floats in the freezing water, another float plane came by, saw the plane upside down in the lake and rescued them. What luck! Apparently the insurance company paid and the plane was abandoned.

Old Scottie, ever conscious of something of value, had located the plane while hunting about 40 km from his camp. It had drifted in to shore and he managed to salvage the fuselage and cache it. Later, during the winter, he had returned to the wreck with his dog team and hauled it back to his camp.

I tried to visualize Scottie driving his dog team along the frozen lake with the fuselage of this plane lashed to his komatik.

'Wouldn't *that* have been a photograph worth taking?' I thought to myself as we headed back down to the lake.

CHAPTER TWENTY-NINE

'Twas the Day Before Christmas

Now my huskies are all stretched out on the ice
And I know that I won't make it home tonight.

Mush Along

S OMETIME DURING THE AFTERNOON, the day before Christmas Eve,1971, Jacob Ikeeneelee came into the office. He stayed around visiting which was unusual, for Jacob was a quiet person and when he wasn't out trapping and hunting he spent his time at home. He was well respected by all the clans in Baker Lake. This was the main reason he was elected the leader of the Hunters and Trappers Association. He got along with everyone.

I was pretty sure Jacob wanted to talk about something or other, but it would have been impolite to ask questions. I knew he would speak when he was ready. He had been talking to Barnabus and after a pause Barnabus said to me. 'Ikeeneelee, maybe he got lots of meat cached.' Barnabus reached in his shirt pocket to replenish the Copenhagen in his lower lip. When this was completed he continued, 'Ikeeneelee say he be pretty happy to get some meat for Christmas.'

I sensed what was coming and my heart sank. Of all the people in Baker Lake, I did not want to refuse a request by Jacob but to think of making a trip on the land so close to Christmas; I slumped in my chair at the thought of it. Jacob must have sensed my reluctance for his smile vanished and he studied my face intently. Again Barnabus spoke. 'Meat not far he say. Maybe we go, come back one day.'

I remained silent for several minutes as my mind digested the idea of another trip, then pointed to the wall map beside my desk.

'*Nami?*' (where?) I said to Jacob. His finger went to the map north of Baker Lake near the north end of Whitehills Lake.

'*Tavvani,*' he said as the smile returned to his face. I reckoned it was about 40 km from the settlement. With a little bit of luck we could make it out and back by suppertime. But what if we broke down? The weather could catch us. I glanced out the window at the fading light. The weather had been fairly decent; cold with ice fog and moderate winds. I turned to Jacob who stood expectantly beside the wall-map, then spoke to Barnabus.

'Tell him we go tomorrow; early, as soon as we can find our way.' I knew we would need every precious minute of daylight. At best we could only hope for six hours.

Iris was incredulous when I told her of my plan.

'You're going on the land the day before Christmas?' she asked in disbelief.

'I couldn't say no. They give caribou meat as gifts and Jacob has never asked me for anything before. Anyway, it's only a day trip, we should be back by supper time.'

Iris didn't reply, but her eyes spoke for her. She knew as well as I that there was a good chance I could break down in the Bombardier. After a pause, I concluded by saying, 'I know I'm taking a chance, but I said I'd get his meat for him and I have to go.'

It was still dark the next morning when I headed down to the garage to get the Bombardier ready for the trip. I tried unsuccessfully to avoid Roy, the head mechanic.

'You're going out today?' he asked in a questioning voice as I opened the door to back out.

'It's just a short trip,' I replied confidently and began to move the Bombardier outside.

The weather was holding, the wind was moderate from the north and the pale halo in the southeast indicated the long-delayed sun was planning a later appearance. Overhead the constellations stood out in the velvet blackness with vivid brightness. Jacob and Barnabus had arrived and everything was ready to go. The east had lightened a little and I asked Barnabus, 'Maybe okay to see now?'

'Maybe we find,' he replied and with this we got in the idling Bombardier and headed north.

By the time the sun struggled above the horizon, we were rolling along the surface of Whitehills Lake making excellent progress. The wind had swept the ice clear of snow in large patches and we clattered along over the glare ice. Soon we were at the north end of the lake and had to pick a trail through a large rocky area. This slowed us down somewhat but we were soon nearing the area where Jacob had cached the caribou. He watched intently through the windshield directing us to the right or left when necessary. At last he said pointing. '*Taikani!*' (over there).

All I could see was rocks and drifted snow. Jacob began probing the snow with the ice chisel and then began digging. I went over with the shovel and helped him dig. We exposed some large rocks which rested on frozen caribou skins. The laborious work began. The rocks had to be dug

138

out, pried loose and moved to one side. The frozen caribou skins were dug loose with snow-knife and shovel before we finally got to the frozen caribou carcasses underneath. Like everything else Jacob did, this work was done well. There was no way a wolf or wolverine would steal his precious meat without a struggle. I could quickly see that this job was going to take longer than I had thought. It took us over an hour of hard steady work to uncover the meat and load it on the sled. By this time, Jacob had found another of his caches some meters distant and the whole procedure began again. There seemed to be about three or four caribou in each cache.

By the time the second cache was loaded the afternoon was well advanced.

'Maybe one more cache,' said Barnabus. 'Not far.'

'Oh no,' I thought. 'Not another cache. We'll have to go back in the pitch dark.'

I almost wanted to say, leave it and we'll get it some other time, but I knew Jacob needed all his meat and it should be taken in before a wolverine found it. We drove further north several kilometers and Jacob began to search for the last cache. By the time we had it dug out and loaded it was dark. The southwest was a pale white streak and the stars could be seen once again. At last everything was loaded and tarped on the big sled and lashed in place. We started for home following our outward trail.

'This will be all right,' I thought. 'The wind's holding off and the sky is clear. We should be okay as long as I take it slowly and steadily so I don't hit a rock and break something.'

The trail across the land showed up perfectly in the headlights on the Bombardier. I was pulling a heavy load on the sled, but everything seemed to be going well. We began our trip down Whitehills Lake. Now the trail was not so plain to follow, especially when we hit patches of glare ice. The trail became long thin scratches on the ice surface caused by the ski-rods and the track bolts in the rubber tracks.

'I can't lose this trail,' I said out loud. 'If we lose our old trail we're sunk.'

I tried to keep the machine lined up with the marks in the ice, so if I lost them momentarily I would soon pick them up again. I slowed down to a crawl, my eyes straining for the little scratches in the ice. As we progressed down the lake we would hit a patch of snow frozen to the ice and I could relax for a few minutes. It galled me that on this surface we could be rolling along at a good speed even with a heavy load, but because of the ever-present danger of losing sight of our old trail, I was down to 5 kph at times.

On a large patch of glare ice I lost the trail completely and allowed the Bombardier to slide to a stop. We got out and searched in the headlights for any sign of the track. Jacob found it a few meters to the right and we were off again. Another patch of glare ice and we lost the trail again. If only I had known how necessary a clear back-trail was going to prove to be I would have gone along the snow covered edge of the lake. I recalled how happy I was as I drove along the frozen ice surface that morning making a good 30 kph.

We searched in vain for the trail, then got back in the Bombardier. There was no moon or northern lights and except for the little pool of light around the Bombardier, very dark.

'*Namut?*' (where to), I asked almost sarcastically of my companions.

I shut off the lights of the Bombardier and we waited until our eyes became accustomed to the dark. Then we got out and looked down the lake. Slowly the rocky outcroppings along the western shore began to take form. I gazed up at Polaris, the North Star; it was exactly behind us. At least we were still headed in the right direction.

Barnabus and Jacob were conversing together in Inuk-tit-tuut and pointing to the right and left as they attempted to identify the shoreline. The knowledge of the land these men possessed never ceased to amaze me. They knew as I did that it was necessary to hit the south end of the lake in just the right place in order to find our way off the lake through a large rocky area.

'Maybe we go,' Barnabus said after a few minutes.

We crept along the ice with the lights off. The shoreline was dimly visible as a long black hulk off to our right. It was a bit unnerving driving along in the dark but the other option was to camp and wait for daylight a good 16 hours away on Christmas Day. That didn't appeal to me at all.

Jacob and Barnabus studied the lakeshore and we continued to creep closer to the south end of the lake. After a few more minutes we could make out the black outline of the south shore. I flipped the headlights back on. Now if only we could find some indication of where we came through the rocks onto the lake. I noticed a patch of snow off to the left where the headlights were bouncing off a disturbance in the surface. I swung over a bit and there was our old Bombardier track. I let out a whoop that startled Barnabus who had his nose inches from the windshield. He was grinning and he spoke something to Jacob in Inuk-tit-tuut. We were back on the snow and on the trail that would lead us through the rocks and home.

When we arrived in the settlement I drove to Jacob's house and we began to unload the sled. People arrived from nearby houses and there was much good-natured laughter and willing hands to clear the sled. As I turned to leave Jacob came and shook my hand earnestly.

'*Mutna,*' (Thank you) he said. '*Gujannamiiraaluk.*' (Thank you very much) He offered me a gift of meat and I headed for the garage very thankful that I had made an effort to help him. Now he had gifts of meat to give his friends and family. I felt good inside as I trudged home over the high snowdrifts.

Iris heard me coming and had a small tape recorder set up by the kitchen table to record the first words of my joyous homecoming.

'So, how did it go?' she asked cheerily.

Unfortunately, my first words were pretty negative, not at all worthy of recording as I recounted that hours previously I had been sitting in the middle of a dark lake wondering if I would be spending Christmas Eve there.

Iris shut off the tape recorder and put her arms around me.

'At least you're home safe and now we can have Christmas together.'

Our son Kevin was in his high chair banging his dish, wanting his supper. As the tensions of the day slipped away, I realized that I was also very hungry and very tired. Iris lit the candles and we sat down to a festive supper with thankful hearts. I was glad I had tried to help someone on Christmas Eve and told Iris how happy Jacob was when we arrived at his house.

CHAPTER THIRTY

The Inuk who made me Laugh (and Cry)

Mush along my huskies take me home
The old north wind has chilled me to the bone.

Mush Along

MY INUIT ASSISTANT FOR OVER A YEAR was Hugh Ungungai. Numerous references have already been made to him but it is really necessary to describe in more detail our relationship during that time.

As I have already said, I found Hugh to be friendly and helpful. His good humour and easy laughter often helped us through some trying situations. I don't wish to dwell on his weakness, but some incidents I thought quite serious at the time, on looking back, I find quite funny. I could say that Hugh had a careless attitude toward equipment and that would be true, but it is also true that he had a carefree attitude about life in general and could always see the humour in any situation. It was most frustrating for me to balance these positive and negative traits from day to day.

I had already noticed Hugh's cavalier attitude and determined not to let equipment fall into his hands without supervision. The first incident that I found most upsetting was the night Hugh came to the house and asked if he could borrow the Bombardier tent. Now I regarded this tent as one of my most prized pieces of equipment. It was made of heavy canvas sewn exactly in the shape of the Bombardier snowmobile. It had heavy gauge zippers on the driver's door and zipper flaps covering the engine compartment doors. Out on the land the tent would completely cover the Bombardier, keeping out the wind and snow. With a Coleman gas stove burning inside, the interior of the Bombardier was quite livable. The best part was the fact that you didn't have to struggle at the end of the day putting up a tent in the howling wind or engage in the time-consuming task of building an igloo.

When Hugh asked to borrow this tent I immediately said no. Hugh persisted. It was a very windy cold night and Hugh couldn't get his Skidoo snowmobile started. If I would just let him use the big tent-tarp he could cover his machine and heat it up so it would start. The very thought of Hugh with a blowtorch and my precious Bombardier tent sent shivers up my spine.

'No way, Hugh,' I said. 'Go borrow a tarp from someone else.'

Reluctantly Hugh left.

I was a little surprised about 40 minutes later to hear the fire siren go off for the settlement. Before long the tracked Muskeg tractor fire truck was chugging in the direction of the office building, red dome lights flashing.

Being somewhat curious, I pulled on my parka and went down to see what was going on. I was relieved to see as I approached that the office building didn't appear to be burning. The smoke was coming from a Skidoo snowmobile parked nearby. 'Hugh's new Skidoo,' I thought. 'He burned it up trying to start it.' As I walked closer I saw the firemen directing a stream of water at a smoldering piece of canvas – green canvas; oh no, that couldn't be my Bombardier tent! But it was, or what was left of it. Anger flashed within me and I began searching through the curious on-lookers for Hugh. He was nowhere to be found. John Tapatai was one of the firemen and also a mechanic at the Government garage.

'Where's Hugh?' I asked.

John grinned and said, 'I think he took off when he saw you coming.'

I examined the burned shreds of canvas. The Bombardier tent was totally useless.

I eventually found out what happened. Hugh had put a blowtorch inside the Skidoo canopy so the flame was directed on to the engine muffler. This he had hoped would heat the motor. Because of the wind, he took the Bombardier tent, without permission, and put it over the whole machine. Instead of staying around to watch, he decided to go visiting while the engine warmed. A gust of wind buffeted the canvas tipping the blowtorch sideways so the flame was directed toward a plastic fuel line. Poof! No more new Skidoo and no more Bombardier tent.

Hugh wisely stayed out of sight for several days, then came in to apologize and offered to pay for the tent.

I was planning to take the Boy Scout troop out to the cabins at Kazan River for a field trip. Several Inuks had agreed to go along and teach the boys how to build an igloo, set fox traps and the like. I knew there would be a lot to get ready on Monday morning so I tried to impress upon Hugh before he left work on Friday how important it would be for him to get to work on time on Monday.

'I'll come to work early,' he assured me. 'I'm not even going out hunting or anything, so I'll be there for sure.'

'Good,' I said. 'I'll be counting on you.' And so we parted for the weekend.

Hugh Ungungai and Scottie Tooloolee.

Hugh was chronically late for work; he just couldn't seem to get going in the morning. I would phone Jean, his wife and ask for him.

'He's still sleeping,' was her stock answer.

'Go wake him up,' I would say.

Once she replied, 'I can't wake him up; he fights me.'

I was sure Hugh's sleeping habits must be pathological.

I went to work early Monday and by 8 a.m. ten rambunctious boys showed up ready for a trip on the land. Hugh was nowhere to be seen. I began sorting out the gear and loading the sled by myself, getting more annoyed at Hugh with each passing moment. The adult hunters arrived and helped me get everything loaded. By 8:45 we were ready to hit the trail. I went into the office and phoned Hugh's number. No one answered. I knew Jean was just letting it ring, so I hung up. The boys crowded into the Bombardier and we headed out across the lake toward the mouth of the Kazan River.

Exactly 30 km down the lake was a large pressure ridge. I found a fair place to cross and after I eased the Bombardier and sled down the other side I decided to get out and check the load. As I rounded the back of the machine, heading for the sled, I jumped back aghast. Something was moving on the top of the front part of the load. It was covered with a thick coating of snow and reminded me of a sled dog who was disturbed while sleeping out a storm.

As I caught my breath, the form took shape and Hugh slid off the snow covered sled and took a step or two forward. He had a broken cigarette clamped in his teeth and he was inspecting his *kamiks* closely. Finally he looked up sheepishly and muttered, 'I tried to light it.' He took the broken cigarette from his mouth and continued, 'But there was too much snow and wind.'

Ignoring his comment I blurted out in amazement. 'Hugh! What the hell are you doing back here?'

Hugh returned to the study of his *kamiks* for several seconds, then looked up again and mumbled, 'I knew you would be pretty mad at me ...' he broke off.

'How did you get back here on the sled?' I asked almost to myself. 'You were nowhere in sight when I left?'

'I knew you'd be pretty mad so when I saw you way down the lake I chased after you with my Skidoo.'

'But where's your Skidoo?' I replied still in shock. 'How did you get on the sled?'

'Well, when I caught up – there was lots of flying snow – well, I just drove as close as I could, shut off my Skidoo and jumped.'

I stood silent for several moments staring at this man, trying to take it all in. I didn't know whether to laugh or cry. Finally a bit of the earlier annoyance returned and I growled, 'Maybe it's safer riding inside.'

Hugh began brushing the snow off his parka and I opened the door to the Bombardier. The boys had stayed inside and when they saw Hugh they clamored, 'Where did he come from?'

'From heaven.' I replied curtly, as I dropped the Bombardier in gear.

On our return journey two days later as we drew close to the settlement I could see Hugh's Skidoo still sitting on the snow about a meter away from my old Bombardier track. I tried to envisage Hugh leaping on the moving sled.

'It must have been much like jumping from a galloping horse to the stagecoach in a Wild West movie,' I thought to myself as I slowed to a stop.

Hugh got out beside his Skidoo.

'That would have been a real photograph,' I expressed as we continued on home.

As we traveled together on the land during my first year in Baker Lake I became well acquainted with Hugh and we got on well together. As long as Hugh didn't have to be anywhere on time or be responsible for equipment, things went along fine.

One night when we were spending an evening in one of our many camps, he told me about a disastrous trip he took by Bombardier with Scottie to Ferguson Lake. There was an abandoned mining camp there and Scottie was the official custodian. This was the winter after Wally Thom had drowned in Baker Lake. Scottie persuaded Hugh to take him down there. It was the same trip that resulted in a big sled and equipment being abandoned near Parker Lake.

They actually made it all the way to Ferguson Lake without breaking down. Being very tired from the long drive Hugh fell asleep in the mine bunkhouse. It was late the next day when Hugh finally realized he had better start the Bombardier. The big Chrysler Industrial V8 wouldn't budge due to the cold and it didn't take Hugh long to run the battery flat trying to start it.

'It was really cold and I was stuck,' Hugh explained, 'and it was only a few days until Christmas.'

Hugh wanted to get home pretty bad. He didn't have a spare battery and although he had taken the Game Management Skidoo snowmobile, he had left it with the big sled and other equipment near Parker Lake.

'We even tried pulling the Bombardier with dogs to get it started,' Hugh explained.

I couldn't help laughing. 'You didn't?'

The idea of pulling a large track vehicle with dogs was quite incredible.

'We tried everything,' Hugh continued, 'but it wouldn't start.'

Hugh persuaded one of the Inuks staying at the camp to take him back by dog team as far as Parker Lake so he could get home by snowmobile before Christmas. They headed out, but a storm blew up and they spent the next three days, including Christmas, sitting in an igloo listening to the wind. After the storm Hugh actually got back to where the Skidoo had been left and headed for Baker Lake at full speed. It would be months before the Bombardier was returned and the scars of Hugh's trip were still very evident. All the wiring on the motor had to be replaced. This was due to Hugh's vain attempts to warm the engine at Ferguson Lake with a two-burner Coleman gas stove. He placed it inside the engine compartment, just below the wiring harness. Luckily there was a fire extinguisher in the machine, otherwise the Bombardier would have suffered the same fate as Hugh's Skidoo.

CHAPTER THIRTY-ONE

Cabins on the Land

I've heard the cry of the Arctic Wolf
Rise up to the frozen stars,
And echo along the trackless snow
That drifts in endless bars.

Home To The Northland

O NE PROJECT, which took a lot of time and effort, was hauling surplus houses to various land camps. I began this work in 1969 and I was still working on it when I was transferred to Inuvik in May of 1971.

The houses were the first units provided to Inuit families who wanted to live in the village and move out of igloos and tents. Several years before I arrived in Baker Lake some families were still living in igloos in winter and tents in summer on the fringe of the settlement. In the fall of 1968, sixty-seven new houses arrived on the ship. Finally there were enough houses for everyone and now some of the old units were vacant. The newly organized Hunters and Trappers Association supported the idea of moving ten to the land camps to be used by people hunting or trapping in the area.

The houses or 'cracker boxes' as they were derogatorily called, were 20 feet by 16 feet. This provided 320 square feet of living space, so the units were officially dubbed '320s'. The roof was almost flat and the units were prefabricated into five four-foot sections, 16 feet long. This made the dismantling, transporting and re-erection quite manageable.

The first two were hauled across the lake by Bombardier and sled and put up near the mouth of the Kazan River, a traditional hunting and fishing site. The hunters and trappers picked all the sites and some of them were many kilometers away from the village. As many as four or five trips were needed by Bombardier and sled to haul one complete house to a site. Except for the cabins at Kazan River, the size was reduced to 16 feet × 16 feet for the other land camps.

One of the most difficult cabins to establish was at the narrows between

Kaminuriak and Parker Lake. The months of April and May were devoted entirely to getting this cabin on site. The weather was bad with storm upon storm rushing out of the north. We would get a good trail broken through and immediately the wind would come up and obliterate all signs. This would mean breaking out a new one with reduced load on the sled.

After several weeks we finally had most of the prefabricated sections cached at the south end of Parker Lake. It was near the end of April and Iris was not happy with the time I had been spending on the land away from home. I thought of a plan to bring peace back to our relationship.

'Why don't you come out to Kazan cabins and stay for a week?' I inquired one morning as I was preparing to leave for work.

'What would I do out there?' she asked, 'You'd still be away all day.'

She had a point. We were using the cabins as a base camp but most of the day was spent freighting the cabin sections to Parker Lake.

'Why don't you ask Gaileen to come along? I'm sure Ron would like an excuse to get out for a while, maybe they can both come.'

At this Iris brightened. Then I added, 'I'll even ask Hugh if he would like to bring Jean along. There are two big cabins out there.'

It wasn't long until we had our plans in place. And so it was around 11 p.m. one evening in late April we pulled out into the lake and headed for Kazan River cabins. On board were Ron and Gaileen Kingdon, our RCMP friends, Hugh, Jean and their two small children, and Iris and I. The sled behind was loaded with fuel and supplies.

I had deliberately delayed our departure until dusk in order to be able to pick up my old trail in the headlights. We rolled along the hard packed trail making good time. At the first big pressure ridge we ran into trouble. I hadn't been over the trail for several days but just assumed nothing had changed. The harsh hand of experience was to teach me a good lesson.

As I approached the high pressure ridge on the old trail everything looked fine. I slowed the Bombardier and shifted into first gear. The technique I had developed to cross these ice ridges with minimal damage to the machine was to run up the incline on one side with enough speed to take the machine to the top of the ridge, then reduce power quickly so the whole outfit would slowly tip over the top and coast down the other side. What I didn't know this night was that the pressure ridge had pulled apart leaving a gap of one meter of open water on the far side. Water had flooded out over the ice leaving a large pond which had not yet frozen.

When the Bombardier started to tip over the top, the headlights flashed down on the pool of floodwater.

'Open water!' I yelled as we bounced down the other side. 'Open the hatch!' I screeched, not knowing how wide the crack had opened. Ron fumbled with the latches on the roof hatch and threw it open. I felt the front skis bounce up on the good ice on the other side of the crack and moments later I felt the back end of the Bombardier drop down. I had traveled a bit on bad ice in Northern Saskatchewan and knew that owing to the heavy motor in the rear, a Bombardier drops through the ice back-end first.

As I felt the back drop, I tramped the gas pedal to the floor hoping the tracks would climb out of the crack. The weight of the sled and load was too much and I killed the engine. I tried starting it again immediately, but the starter whined uselessly.

'Get out!' I yelled. 'Everyone get out!' The door flew open and Hugh began helping Jean and their kids out. Soon we were all standing in 15 centimeters of floodwater.

I half expected the Bombardier to slowly sink into the crack; the back-end had dropped in so far the front skis were suspended in the air. Hugh, Ron and I rushed over to salvage some bedrolls and equipment should this be the case. We were 32 km out on the lake and the night was cold.

After we had retrieved the essentials for survival, I began a closer inspection of the situation with a flashlight. The motor was still clear of the water and by poking around with the ice chisel I was able to determine that things were not as bad as they first appeared. By reaching down into the frigid water I was able to unhook the sled. Then I got in and tried to start the engine. After several futile attempts, it caught. I revved it up and slowly released the clutch. Without the weight of the sled it tracked up easily out of the crack and onto the good ice.

It was a relieved group of people that climbed back inside, wet feet and all. I drove as fast as the trail would allow for the cabins where we would be able to dry our footwear.

'This doesn't happen on every trip,' I said. The faces of the women still reflected concern as we bounced across the drifts.

Tomorrow it would be business as usual as we retrieved the sled from the pressure ridge and continued to haul the cabin sections to Parker Lake.

Spring was long in coming that year. It was already the first week of May and still the wind blew from the north with little reprieve. We were enjoying our camp-out together. I still had several trips to make to complete the job but the end was near.

One stormy day we had decided to stay at the cabins. The day passed slowly as we sat around visiting and drinking tea as the wind whipped the snow to a white froth around the buildings. By evening things improved and someone went out to get ice to melt for water.

'There's a dog team coming,' was the cry and we all went out to greet the unexpected company.

It was Itow's team and he sat near the front directing his dogs. Behind him was a very tall, lanky *Qallunaaq*. He got off and strode over to where we were standing.

'Hello,' I said, 'and who might you be?'

The tall stranger looked around before he replied, 'I'm Ken from Pennsylvania.'

'Well, come in and have some tea,' I replied and turned with the others back to the cabins for more formal introductions.

Ken followed us to our cabin; Itow went with Scottie, Hugh and Jean to the other. Ken, we quickly learned, was quite laconic. He seemed reluctant to provide many details about himself. As we had a snack and drank several cups of tea, he did tell us he had canoed down the Kazan with a party the previous summer from Snowbird Lake in Manitoba. He was quite impressed with Kazan Falls and held out the dream of returning to see the falls in winter. He said he was a mathematician and taught at some college in Pennsylvania.

This fellow seemed a bit different somehow and after I had explained a little about what we were trying to achieve by establishing cabins in traditional Inuit land camps, there was a long structural silence. It was broken by Ken turning to me abruptly and saying, 'I think I understand what you're doing out here,' and then turning to Ron he continued, 'but I'm not sure what you're doing out here?'

Ron looked at me and grinned, then shrugged. Iris and Gaileen looked at each other perplexed. Finally I answered half seriously, 'Maybe he's here to keep an eye on mathematicians from Pennsylvania.' This ended the conversation for the evening and we offered him a piece of the floor to roll out his bedroll. He accepted and began his preparations in silence.

Next morning we watched Itow prepare his komatik for the trip to the falls. He hitched his dogs and the tall mathematician climbed on. With a crack of the dog-whip they were off, the tall *Qallunaaq* looking much out of place behind the diminutive Inuk, Itow.

Hugh told me this was their second night out of the village. Itow built an igloo the first night and spent a difficult time with Ken. Itow didn't speak English and Ken knew nothing of igloo living so they spent a long night. Itow knew we were at the Kazan camp so he headed there for some more amiable company.

'You meet all kinds in the North,' Ron commented.

'You do indeed.' I replied.

The cabin on the Quoich River was hauled in with Tapitai's Peterhead boat in September. It was situated below St. Clair Falls in tidal waters. A beautiful place, with high rolling hills to the west and the roar of the waterfall several kilometers to the northeast. I remember well the morning we began to erect the cabin. We had the floor down and had started hauling the wall sections up from the shore when someone spotted caribou on the west bank. Hugh started for the canoe.

'Whoa, wait a minute. We have a cabin to build here. The caribou aren't going anywhere,' I said.

The animals were grazing peacefully along the shore. Reluctantly everyone went back to work or at least were going through the motions. Every few minutes heads would turn and eyes would gaze across the river. Finally, as work slowed considerably I knew this wasn't going to work.

'*Taima!*' (Enough) I yelled.

All eyes turned my way. I had four workers including Hugh.

I said to Hugh. 'Go kill some caribou, but don't spend the whole day over there!'

His hammer dropped like a stone and a grin flashed on his face.

'*Aullalirta!*' (Let's be leaving) Hugh yelled to the other Inuks as he ran for the canoe. Soon only old Thomas Tapitai and I were left. I sat down on the floor platform to watch the hunt develop on the opposite shore. We would finish the cabin when every caribou in sight was either killed or chased back into the hills.

The cabin we moved to Andrews Lake was south of Christopher Island near the east end of Baker Lake and about 90 km from the settlement. It held many memories for me – not all pleasant. I began hauling the prefabricated sections out in the middle of February, but the cabin wasn't completely finished until April.

The first trip out was to cache fuel and inspect the site for the cabin. We hauled a light load and everything was going fine. After leaving Baker Lake I began following a small stream south which would take us to Andrews Lake. As I was thinking how well things were going, I felt the back of the Bombardier drop, an indication that we were breaking through the ice. The stream was shallow so it wasn't a big worry. When I got stopped on good ice we all got out to check for damage. The Bombardier was fine but not so the bobsled following behind. The runners on the rear half of the sled had dropped into the hole made by the Bombardier track and the runners were broken. The stream had frozen, then the water drained away leaving a large air pocket to trap unaware travelers.

The second trip to Andrews Lake is the one I remember best of all. A huge pressure ridge had developed running almost all the way across the east end of Baker Lake. It was six meters high in places and it took a lot of searching to find a place to cross. I needed enough speed to get up to the top of the ridge then I had to cut power quickly so the front end didn't come down too hard on the other side. I thought we had done well, but

Quoich River cabin. 12 passenger Bombardier snowmobile pulling sled.

when I inspected for damage on the other side I found the shock absorber was broken off. All that held the ski in place now was a metal bracket with a rubber bumper designed to reduce the pressure on the shock absorber in the downward movement of the ski.

I should have turned and headed for home but we were over half way to our destination so I decided to reduce speed and try to deliver our load. It took longer to get there but we made it without further incident. The next day was spent completing the assembly of the cabin.

I had developed the habit of carrying a small barometer with me on the land. I found that any rapid movement of the needle up or down brought strong winds in about six to eight hours. On the morning of the second day I noticed the needle on the barometer had moved rapidly downward a considerable gradient. I told Barnabus that we would be leaving for home right away. There were four of us in the party and we packed up quickly and headed northwest toward Baker Lake. Not wanting to cross the high pressure ridge again with a broken shock absorber, I went north across Baker Lake hoping the pressure ridge ended before reaching the north shore. Luck was not with us; the ridge of ice ran right in to the shore and then followed the shoreline west a few meters from the steep rocky bank. There was no place to get up off the ice and go around. I picked the best place I could find on that ridge of ice and drifted snow and attempted to cross. Without being sure just how I managed it, a few minutes later I had the Bombardier over on one side stuck tight against a great blue-green slab of lake-ice. We were in a mess and I knew it. To add to our torment the wind began to pick up and soon we were working with shovels, ice chisels and jack-all in a swirling ground-drift.

The sled was dropped, the Bombardier jacked back level and a path chopped and shoveled through that miserable pressure ridge. I noticed that the metal bracket and rubber bumper were completely sheared off. Now nothing restricted the downward travel of the ski. When we had done all we could do to level a path through, I motioned everyone inside. After we warmed up a bit, I put the machine in gear and revved up the engine. This was no time to be gentle; I had to have all the momentum possible to get up and over that jumble of ice. The clutch was released and I applied power. We bounced, jerked and bumped forward with the tracks spinning until we were up and over. In the process the ski dropped down with nothing to restrain it and the big heavy coil spring rolled out on the ice. We jacked up the front-end and put the spring back in place. This was a task we would repeat many times in the next ten hours.

The wind increased in fury, straight from the north as we crept along the ice following the north shore of the lake. I was driving into a blinding wall of white. Darkness fell as we continued on at about 10 kph. If I increased the speed on the uneven drifts the ski would drop down and the coil spring would fall out. Then we had to jack up the front and put it back. Sometimes it seemed we covered several kilometers before it fell out, other times it seemed we only went a few hundred meters. The wind drove the snow granules like bits of sand into our faces, sucking the very breath from our tired lungs. Feverishly we worked to get the spring in place and get back inside.

I thought of calling a halt and waiting the storm out but that could be three or four days. The blow was just beginning. No – as long as we were capable of making forward progress, we would keep going.

I lost track of how many times we had to get out and jack up the front to replace the spring. I could no longer see the north shore as darkness fell. Barnabus directed me to keep driving so the force of the wind was hitting us directly on the right side. Coming out of the north this would keep us going west.

After many hours of this tortuous routine we came to a large patch of glare ice. I had the skis cramped as far as they would go to the right and yet the wind gusts were pushing the front end of the Bombardier around. The ski rods slid sideways on the glare ice and there was nothing we could do about it. Soon we were almost heading downwind. I had to stop, back up and drive back directly into the wind for some distance before turning broadside to the wind again. Slowly the wind began to push the front end around. I can't recall how often I had to repeat this procedure before we were back on hard-packed snow. The ski rods contacted the hard snow again and we were able to maintain our westerly direction.

Alex Ilkat, an Inuk who helped assemble the houses and a chronic complainer, began to argue with Barnabus in Inuk-tit-tuut. I asked Eddie Adams who could speak English fluently what the problem was?

He said, 'Alex thinks we're going in the wrong direction.'

I dismissed this outright. I had traveled great distances under similar conditions and had complete confidence in Barnabus and his ability to navigate in a storm. I kept driving into a white wall of blinding snow, cutting the wind as squarely to 90 degrees as I was capable.

Ten torturous hours later I almost ran into a runway marker on the ice strip beside the village. We knew we had made it home once more.

When I got to my house, I pulled off my heavy clothes with Iris' help. I could hardly move my arms; the result of so many hours hunched over the steering wheel peering through a small round hole in the frosted windshield. This was all the defroster was capable of keeping clear in the extreme cold. I was so glad to be home. I lay on the floor and Iris massaged my aching neck and arms. Kevin was disappointed that I was not paying attention to him and he sat down on me in annoyance. Outside our warm house the wind shrieked incessantly and would continue for a full 48 hours. I was so glad we were waiting out the storm here and not cramped in a frigid Bombardier down the lake.

We established a cabin on a small river that drained the east end of a large lake 80 km west of the settlement. It was February when we began making trips to the lake. It was an excellent place for a camp midway between Baker and Beverly Lakes. This made it a good stopping place for hunters and trappers traveling to that area.

The big lake had been named by the Inuit eons before the *Qallunaaq* arrived, but it did not have a name assigned by the Government's Surveys and Mapping branch. This changed shortly after we began building the cabin. I read in a newspaper that this lake had been named after Justice John H. Sissons of the Northwest Territories Superior Court. The Inuit called him *Ekoktoegoe* (the one who listens to things) and he was well known across the north as one who tried to mete out white man's justice with some appreciation of the native culture.

As we were having tea in our newly completed cabin, I told Hugh that this lake had been named after Justice Sissons. Hugh said he had heard of him, then added, 'He's the judge who gave back Matthew's $200.00.'

Matthew Koonungnak was with us on this trip and after Hugh had talked to him for awhile in Inuk-tit-tuut, a grin spread over Matthew's face. I remembered reading a report in the office about Matthew killing a muskox and being fined by Barry Gunn, the Area Administrator for Baker Lake and also the Justice of the Peace for the settlement.

'Why did they give him back his fine?' I asked Hugh. 'I heard it was because the muskox was chasing him or his family.'

Hugh took the cigarette from his lips and started laughing.

'It was Matthew who was chasing the muskox,' he said, then translated for Matthew. Soon they were both laughing. Matthew had reported the killing of the muskox himself when he returned from his camp and the RCMP laid the charge. There was no Game Officer assigned to Baker Lake at this time, although Barry Gunn held the appointment so he could sign licences and forms.

Justice Sissons had quashed the conviction, ruling that Matthew was just protecting his family and on the technical point that Gunn couldn't be a JP and Game Officer at the same time. Overlooking the technical point it seemed to me that justice had been dispensed in the first instance. Matthew knew he shouldn't have killed the muskox and because of his honest nature had reported it, expecting to be fined. What followed in *Regina Versus Koonungnak* was more confusion about the *Qallunaaq* and his strange way of doing things. At least they were getting a good laugh over it.

As far as the name of the lake was concerned, the Inuit would continue calling it by the name assigned long ago by their Forefathers, regardless of names printed on a map.

CHAPTER THIRTY-TWO

White-out and Survival

And I wondered what power in the world of men
Could draw my feet to stand
From the gentle south, to a land as harsh
And cruel as this northern land.

Home To The Northland

IT IS DIFFICULT FOR ANYONE to understand the effect of 'white-out' conditions in the Arctic without actually experiencing them. It is also very hard to describe the phenomenon accurately. It is however a common condition, especially in the months of March and April when the sun is high and the sky is overcast. Many travelers have lost their way or hurt themselves while challenging such conditions. Simply put, the horizon disappears due either to blowing snow or changing light conditions or a combination of the two and all references to ground and sky are lost. You find yourself in a great dimensionless white void.

Late in April of 1971, I received word that an Inuk was missing from a camp north of Baker Lake near Whitehills Lake. He had lost his way in a 'white-out' returning to his igloo from an ice-fishing hole. Barnabus and I joined others in the search for the missing man. He had not returned to the camp after two days and his family was concerned.

When I saw the fishing hole the man had left to return to the igloo less than 50 meters away, it was difficult to imagine how he could have missed it, but of course I was standing on the ice in bright sunshine. Remembering the times I had been caught in the white-out phenomenon, I knew it was very easy to do.

The search ranged far and wide across Whitehills Lake, but no sign of the missing fisherman could be found. Late that afternoon with the Bombardier running low on fuel we reluctantly turned back on the tracks we had made on our outward journey. In my mind I pictured another frozen body drifted over with snow.

As we rolled along the trail back to Baker Lake, Barnabus grabbed my arm: '*Taku*,' meaning look, then added pointing, '*taikani*,' (over there). What I saw were footprints in the snow, very close together, intercepting our Bombardier tracks. We climbed out for a closer look. Someone, obviously near the end of their physical endurance, had shuffled along until stepping down into the trough made by the Bombardier track in a patch of soft snow suddenly stopped. We could see where the person had crawled along a little way, then got to his feet and continued walking following the track south toward the settlement. His steps were short and methodical.

'Plenty tired,' Barnabus said looking at the tracks.

'*Ii*,' I replied in the affirmative, then added, '*Piunngittug*' (it's bad). 'Maybe he can't see so good.'

'*Ii*,' Barnabus replied.

We realized from his actions on his hands and knees that he was almost snow-blind and had fallen to his knees to inspect the Bombardier track before following it.

We jumped back in the Bombardier and I drove as fast as the rough terrain would allow in the hope that we would catch up to the Inuk before he collapsed. We were still five or so kilometers from the settlement.

Happily he made it all the way on his own following the tracks. He was indeed almost snow-blind and totally exhausted but at least he had survived.

In December of the same year, Hugh Ooshulook had not been so fortunate. He had lost the battle with fatigue and cold, though not because of a white-out. He had been on a hunting trip in this same area of Whitehills Lake with John Iqsakittouk when their snowmobile had broken down. They were stranded about 40 km north of the village. They made a camp and spent the first night on the land. They didn't have the means to repair the snowmobile, so early next day they began to walk home. It was very cold but at least the cold north wind was at their backs.

As the day progressed, the wind increased and soon they were walking in blowing snow. Hugh was having trouble keeping up. They were still ten or more kilometers from the settlement when Hugh became totally exhausted and could not go on. John gave him the snow-knife and told him to make a shelter while he went on for help. John told me later that after he left Hugh and had gone on a short way, he looked back and saw him down on his knees with the snow-knife sticking in the snow in front of him.

I remember well the frantic search we embarked on that night in storm and darkness after John struggled home. The area north was very rocky and Barnabus helped me pick a route through with the Bombardier. Others went out with their snowmobiles to aid in the search. The temperature and wind-chill was severe.

Hugh was found by one of the searchers but it was too late to save his life. His frozen body was lying right where John had last seen him kneeling. The snow-knife was still sticking in the snow. He hadn't the strength to cut the first block for a shelter.

As I looked at his frozen form I could see that his *kamik* had come apart at the seams and he had been walking in his wool duffel sock. I was deeply saddened by his death, because it seemed so unnecessary. Before the advent of the *Qallunaaq* and his machines, these men would have been hunting with a dog team. Their dogs would not have left them stranded. I determined to try to rekindle some interest in keeping more working dog teams in Baker Lake. Their dogs had been a unique breed, second to none in the Arctic, and now other breeds were being mixed and the number of teams declining.

The summer of 1970 brought considerable exploration activity to Baker Lake. The search for minerals is by nature a secretive endeavor, and despite the continuous arrival and departure of all types of aircraft and crew, no one in the settlement really knew who was searching for what or where the activity was centered. Frequent rumours kept our coffee breaks interesting.

Jim Hamilton was a helicopter pilot who was in and out of the village a lot that summer. He was flying for Athabasca Airways, a company I had frequently chartered while working in northern Saskatchewan. I chatted with him whenever I had an opportunity. We had several mutual friends flying for the Airways.

I was away on the land when Jim departed around the last week of September en route to Prince Albert Saskatchewan via Ennadai Lake. Michel Lindhaler was cooking at the Department of Transport kitchen and remembered the morning Jim left. Michel had kindly prepared a substantial box-lunch for Jim and he almost left without it. Michel heard he was about to lift off and ran out with the lunch and flagged him down. He had no way of knowing that his generous lunch would be instrumental in saving Jim's life in the ensuing weeks.

Jim Hamilton failed to arrive at the Ennadai Weather Station. Before long the news got back to Baker Lake and the Armed Forces Search and Rescue Aircraft began their work. Those who knew Jim were deeply concerned. The weather had been quite stormy after he left Baker Lake, and we all hoped he was just waiting it out somewhere. As days stretched into weeks anxiety for his safety heightened.

Athabasca Airways had several aircraft working out of Baker Lake on the search. I wasn't surprised when Jim Monroe, another pilot friend from Prince Albert, arrived. We spent one evening visiting but the ongoing search cast a somber cloud over us. It was over two weeks since Jim disappeared and Munroe didn't think there was much hope he would be found alive. After the third week search activity ceased. Winter was returning to the Keewatin and the days were growing visibly shorter.

Ennadai Lake is 440 kilometers southwest of Baker Lake. If someone threw a gob of paint at a wall it would probably look much like the outline of the lake. The Weather Station is located almost halfway down a boot-like peninsula on the northeast extremity of the lake.

On 25 October word reached us that Jim Hamilton had walked in to the Ennadai Weather Station. We couldn't believe it. 'I'll bet you Jim will have quite a story to tell,' I commented to Iris as we sat in the living room after receiving the news.

'Did they say what kind of shape he was in?'

'I didn't get many details; they just said he was pretty hungry, but in fair condition considering what he had been through. It'll be quite a story, you can count on that.'

Some time would elapse before I was able to get Jim's story through my friends at Athabasca Airways. Another example of indomitable self-reliance could now be added to the annals of the north.

As Jim flew southwest over innumerable lakes that cover the area between Yathkyed and Ennadai Lakes, he experienced the capriciousness of late September weather. He was beyond the 'point of no return' so he knew his only hope was to try to find the Weather Station. With fuel almost gone he finally landed the helicopter and began the long wait for rescue. He waited two weeks and never heard the sound of a Search and Rescue Aircraft. In the interim Jim had a lot of time to think. He studied his track south on his maps and determined that he must have over-flown Ennadai Lake. Jim would draw on his many years of experience as he warmed the engine and managed to restart the machine. He was determined to fly back north as far as his meager fuel supply would take him, land the helicopter, and set out for the Weather Station on foot.

He did all of that and more. He arrived at what he was certain was the shore of Ennadai Lake. In typical character he vowed he would walk all the way around it if necessary until he found the Weather Station. He had been rationing his food since first landing, including Michel's life-sustaining lunch. Freeze-up had taken place and Jim was able to travel on the lake ice which aided his progress. Day after day he struggled along the shoreline. All his food was gone and he was growing weaker.

The morning of 25 October was clear and cold as Jim trudged along the rocky shore. He rounded a small point and on the northeast shore the radio towers of the Weather Station were prominent against the sky. Later recounting the moment Jim would say, 'When I saw those towers I let out a yell loud enough for everyone there to hear me.'

One of the men manning the Station noticed a small black form out on the ice. At first he thought it was a caribou, but it didn't act like one. The black shape would move a short distance then appear to lie down on the ice. After several minutes it would get up and continue moving. Binoculars identified the form of a man who could only walk a short distance before resting. Men grabbed their parkas and headed down to the lake. The man on the ice was Jim Hamilton.

Several months later we received news more incredulous than this. Jim Hamilton had collapsed and died of a heart attack in his mother's living room in Vancouver.

CHAPTER THIRTY-THREE

Arctic Tomfoolery

And then I remembered the gentle moods
And the rivers swift and strong,
Of August winds on a changing page
Where far off lines linger on.

Home To The Northland

AFTER LIVING IN A REMOTE Arctic settlement for a while, it became apparent that many of the residents possessed the propensity for prankish behavior. Whether this trait developed as a natural means of compensating for the isolation or the long Arctic night I could not determine, but I soon found that I was not immune.

I have already mentioned some of the tricks attempted on us on our wedding night, but it went far beyond that. There were stories of many mischievous occurrences perpetrated on unsuspecting residents. A man returned from annual leave to find his house interior completely painted a bright pink. A recently wed couple returned home to find an inflated weather balloon filling the interior of their bedroom. Once inflated the only means of removal was to puncture the balloon. It was filled with flour and rice crispies which the exploding rush of air spread throughout the room. One had to be constantly alert. It didn't pay to provide a prankster with an opportunity for a trick. New arrivals were especially vulnerable. I tried to keep my pranks within the bounds of good taste but I could not resist a good opportunity when it came my way.

It was April first and the sun was already high in the sky as the settlement began to awaken. I stood in the living room looking out at the cold clear morning. Yves Vezina's house was directly in front of ours but further down the slope to the lake.

'You know,' I shouted to Iris in the kitchen. 'We should play a joke on Yves. After all, it is April Fool's Day.'

'I can't think of anything right now,' she replied.

161

I stood looking at his house racking my brain. 'I think I have something,' I exclaimed.

'What?' she asked.

'You know what a hunting and fishing fanatic he is?'

'Yes, but what ...'

I cut her off. 'Just stay here and watch his back door.'

Iris gave me a perplexed look as I ran to the phone. I dialed Yves' number and let it ring. I knew he and his wife would still be in bed on this frigid Saturday morning. Finally the receiver was lifted and I heard a sleepy 'Hello?'

I replied in the most serious but hushed tone possible. 'Yves; this is Ellis. Listen, I just looked out the window and there's a big Arctic hare right by the garbage barrel by your back door.'

His reply was immediate and excited. 'It's just out the back door?'

'Yes! now listen; get your rifle and sneak out the door real quiet because he's just sitting there and you'll be able to get him for sure!'

'Gee, thanks for letting me know.'

The receiver clicked. I rushed back to the living room to watch the fun.

'You're real mean, you know,' Iris said, but she was grinning in anticipation.

In less than a minute the barrel of a rifle appeared through the porch door. Yves followed crouched low, walking carefully. He was dressed only in his pajamas. 'He's going to freeze,' Iris remarked sympathetically.

'Now there's a picture of a dedicated hunter,' I replied laughing.

Yves slowly peered around the garbage barrels and scanned the area. He stood up and cast an inquiring stare toward our house. We waved and clapped, jumping up and down in front of the window laughing. Yves shook his fist at us and stalked back inside.

'I'll phone him later and remind him it's April Fool's Day.'

'I'm sure he knows,' Iris replied, still laughing. 'Did he ever look funny creeping out in his pajamas.'

The best opportunity for a trick came just before I was scheduled to be transferred to Inuvik. I was hauling a surplus house north to the Sandhills camp and was returning home one afternoon. I had made several trips and the trail was packed, frozen and in good condition. In some stretches I could achieve 50 kph.

As I crested the top of a hill about 15 km from Baker Lake I could see the Water Resource's Muskeg tractor chugging along my trail several kilometers ahead of me. They had a small shack on Kingyouk Creek where they were monitoring the stream flow and were now returning from one of their periodic visits. I knew they wouldn't hear me over the sound of their machine, so I decided to give them a good scare.

I was pulling my large empty bob-sled behind which combined with the tracks of the Bombardier sent a blizzard of snow in all directions. I thought, 'If I can get up enough speed, I'll come right up behind them, then suddenly swing out into the deep snow and go around; the noise of the Bombardier and the flying snow should send them right off their seats.' I laughed derisively as I tramped the accelerator to the floor. Barnabus, sitting in the passenger's seat, had just reached into his pocket to replenish his snuse. He cast an inquiring glance at me as he hurriedly shoved his Copenhagen box back and grabbed the edges of his seat. I knew he was probably thinking I had finally 'lost it' but if I was going to make this work I didn't have time to explain.

Going down slope on a packed trail was easy. I was up to 60 kph as I approached unseen behind the Muskeg tractor. I could see Enar and Joe in the cab looking straight ahead as they toddled along at 15 kph. Barnabus had both feet braced against the floorboards as he held his seat with both hands. Mere meters behind, going at top speed I suddenly swung off the trail to the left and hit the snow. This slowed the Bombardier somewhat but our momentum carried us past and I then swung back on the trail right in front of them. A glance in the mirror revealed a violent cloud of snow expanding in every direction.

I slowed down a bit and yelled to Barnabus. 'Those guys plenty scared!' He gave me a nervous grin and loosened his grip on the sides of the seat.

That night was movie night at the community hall. Iris and I arrived late and took our places near the back. The hall was always full. Midway on the left side sat Enar Engstrom with his wife. I looked around and spotted Joseph Keauyuk before the lights went out and the show started. I wondered how badly I had scared them. The first movie reel ended and the lights came on. I kept a low profile. People were lining up at the concession booth. I waited and when I saw Enar go up I slipped up behind him. He turned to see who was waiting next to him. I was ready. 'Hi Enar, say, didn't I see you somewhere out on the land this afternoon?'

He took a playful swing at me with his fist, and uttered an expletive. 'You put Joe and me right through the roof! We thought our engine had exploded.'

I laughed heartily. 'I couldn't pass up a chance like that.'

'Just wait, I'll get you.'

'Better do it quick, I'm getting transferred out in May!'

When I returned to my seat, Iris asked, 'Is he really mad at you?'

'Naw,' I said. 'But I sure scared him. He'll be looking over his shoulder for a while when he's driving to Kingyouk Creek!'

CHAPTER THIRTY-FOUR

Hunting on the Quoich

Oh lonely shores that echo to
The laughter of the loon
Oh restless lakes that shimmer
Beneath the silver moon
Wherever I may wander
And wherever I may roam
I know up there in the Northland
I'll always find a home.

Northern Journey

ONE AFTERNOON I WAS WALKING ALONG the beach of Baker Lake when I decided to inspect a large open boat pulled up on shore. It had been there a long time but I hadn't taken the time to look at it closely. The motor was missing but the hull was in good condition. It appeared to have been used very little. 'This would be an excellent craft for the large unprotected waters of Baker Lake,' I thought as I gave it a thorough inspection. 'I could haul fuel and cabin material and the hunters and trappers could use it for fishing.' I decided to find out all I could about the boat.

I quickly learned that the Government owned it. It had been delivered several years earlier, used to assist the unloading of the supply ship and then hauled out for the winter. As far as anyone knew, it had not been used again. The fate of the motor was a mystery. If anyone knew what happened to it, they were keeping it to themselves. The boat had been built in Nova Scotia, was about nine meters long and designed for the open sea. It was a shame that such a practical and useful craft had been so carelessly abandoned. I was determined to get it back in service, but in order to do this a suitable motor had to be found.

I decided to discuss the boat with Murray Graves, who had recently replaced Roy Emery as the chief government mechanic. I knew he was from the Maritimes and probably knew a lot about boats. I wasn't disappointed.

'Why don't you pull that little Lister diesel out of that tub that's out in the lake and put it to good use.' He was referring to a large pleasure-type government boat which was anchored just off the beach. It was named *Diana* and seemed to be of no practical use. The reason it had been shipped here in the first place was buried in government files.

'Sounds okay to me,' I replied. Murray was one who hated red tape and went straight to a problem and fixed it without asking questions.

'When I get clear of my work in the garage, I'll have a look and see if I can match it up with that trap boat.'

True to his word, Murray checked things out and reassured me that the motor could be installed with a few modifications. It didn't take him long to get the job done either. I asked Pauli, the government carpenter, to build a cabin over the engine and a small wheelhouse. He did an excellent job. In a much shorter time that I ever expected, the boat was in the water. I took it for a test run and everything worked smoothly. I found a file on the boat in the office and learned it had been named the *Nowja*, meaning seagull in Inuk-tit-tuut.

I started putting plans in place to transport some stove oil to Quoich River cabin in the *Nowja*. This would save a lot of hauling by Bombardier. In a small village news gets around quickly and before long Bob Murphy, the RCMP Corporal, had dropped in and asked to go along. He had been trying for most of the summer to get a trip on the land. Boris Kotelewetz got wind of the impending trip and wondered if I had room for him. I agreed since I needed a crew and even with freight the boat could comfortably accommodate three of us.

The following morning we weighed anchor and I nosed the *Nowja* toward the east end of the lake. It would take two days travel to reach the cabin on the Quoich.

We spent a comfortable first night at the soapstone quarry cabin two-thirds of the way down the lake. The weather was moderate and the lake smooth. We made an early departure on the second day and as the morning progressed we passed along the northern tip of Christopher Island. I had read somewhere that this large island had been named in honour of Captain William Christopher who sailed a Hudson's Bay Company vessel up Chesterfield Inlet to the lake in 1761. I wondered if the land had changed much since then. I scanned the rugged island landscape as we chugged eastward.

We found the entrance to the North Channel without difficulty and were soon skimming between the steep rocky outcropping in bright sunshine. The channel narrowed between a small island and I was surprised to see white water ahead. I didn't have tide tables and now it was obvious that we were going through at low tide. I felt the current grab the *Nowja* like a clenching fist. We surged forward; the current was too strong to turn back. I steered the boat away from the foamy white crests into the oily-smooth surge of the main channel. In less than a kilometer we were through the surf and back in the wider channel. I looked at my watch and made a mental note. We would have to catch the high tide on our return if we hoped to make it through.

As we sailed along, the passing scenery was spectacular. Brilliant sunbeams danced across the dappled surface of the blue-green water. The smell of salt was in the air. The steep rocky cliffs displayed a colored mosaic of orange, brown and gray and on ledges and plateaus the surface was green and red where Arctic heather, dwarf-birch and lichens had gained a foothold.

We skirted the islands that marked the entrance to Cross Bay keeping the north shore in sight. I didn't want to sail past the mouth of the wide bay into which the Quoich River drained.

It soon became apparent as we traveled up the narrowing bay which ended below St. Claire Falls, that we would be hard-pressed to make it to the cabin before dark. I anxiously scanned ahead with binoculars searching for the little square cabin in the failing light. A curious seal surfaced near the boat, submerged, only to surface again moments later.

Just before it appeared darkness would overtake us we spotted the cabin on the darkening shore. Blackness came quickly as I maneuvered the *Nowja* to what appeared to be a safe distance offshore. Bob prepared to drop the anchor. We needed a flashlight to see as we loaded the canoe and paddled to the rocky beach. A flat rock ledge provided a good place to haul up the canoe.

It didn't take us long to get ourselves comfortably established in the cabin. Soon the Coleman stove was hissing as water heated for tea. We leisurely consumed our evening meal and drew lots for the bunk. Boris and I would have to take the floor. I hadn't realized how tired I felt until I stretched out on the plywood. Within minutes I was asleep.

I awoke suddenly to the sound of someone shouting my name. I sat up and looked around. The room was still quite dark but I could make out the form of Bob standing on the bunk peering out the small window below the ceiling. His booming voice filled the room again.

'Ellis! Wake up! The boat's sunk!'

I blinked in disbelief, then leapt to my feet almost tumbling over in the attempt to extricate myself from my sleeping robe. I stumbled to the large window above the table and looked out. In the faint light of dawn I could see the bow of the *Nowja* straining at the anchor rope in a strong gale.

Only the bow and the top of the wheelhouse were visible; the rest was submerged beneath the churning waves.

I uttered an expletive and said, 'I wonder how that happened?'

Bob lit a match as he climbed down from the bunk.

'I just woke up,' he exclaimed, 'and decided to have a look out. I couldn't believe my eyes.'

I fumbled around in the dark for my flashlight. By now Boris had been roused by the commotion and the three of us went down to the water. I shone the flashlight along the bow to where it disappeared under the waves.

'At least there's enough wood in her to keep afloat,' I said as I tried to grapple with the magnitude of our problem.

'Before the tide turns we'll have to haul her up as high as we can so we can bail her at low tide.'

My companions agreed.

'It will be daylight in an hour; let's go make a pot of coffee,' Bob suggested. 'There's nothing we can do for a while.'

We retreated to the cabin and lit the lantern.

After several cups of hot coffee, bannock and jam, we returned to the shore and launched the canoe. After paddling out to the submerged *Nowja* we attached another line and attempted to haul up the anchor. It was jammed in the rocky bottom and required a lot of work to get it free. We took the bowline to shore and heaved on it in our attempt to haul the submerged vessel in. It took all we had to slowly drag the heavy craft closer to shore. We wanted to get it as far up the smooth shelf where we had beached the canoe as possible. We still had a way to go when the keel grounded on the rocky bottom.

'We'll have to get her higher or she'll still be in the water at low tide,' I said as we secured the line to a large rock. We had a 'come-along' winch and quickly rigged it to the bowline. Slowly we inched the boat further up the rock shelf.

'That should be far enough,' Boris said. 'We can bail it when the tide goes out.'

We secured it tightly and returned to the cabin.

As the tide fell, the sun came up clear indicating a beautiful day was on the way. We began the grimy task of bailing the *Nowja*. Diesel fuel had leaked from the tank and coated everything inside the engine compartment. It was an oily mess.

'Why don't we just leave it for a while and go do some hunting?' Bob suggested. 'There's not much more we have to do right now.'

'You guys go hunting if you like,' I replied. 'I'm not going to be able to concentrate on anything else until I get this motor checked out. If there's water in the crankcase, we could be in trouble.'

Bob and Boris departed up-river in search of caribou while I began cleaning up the mess in the boat. The tide was still receding and soon I could see the rudder and propeller. I noticed that a length of plastic rope had wrapped itself around the propeller shaft.

'I thought the boat seemed a little sluggish yesterday,' I thought to myself. 'I'll have to get that off!'

I pulled out my knife and slid along the rock shelf and under the stern of the boat. It was a tight squeeze and as I cut away at the rope I was suddenly seized by acute panic. 'What if I can't get out from under here? If the boat shifts I'll be pinned here with the tide coming in and no one to help.' I fought the panic and kept hacking at the rope. Pieces began to fall away and soon I had it clear. I began to wiggle back up the rock shelf fighting panic all the way. I stood up exhausted, wet and gasping for air. I sat down on a flat rock to rest.

As I rested on the boulder I looked down the broad expanse of the Quoich to the opposite shoreline. Everything looked so beautiful in the bright morning sun. It was hard to match the beauty of the tundra in late August. The blue of the river blended peacefully with the rugged rocky shore sloping upward with patches of multi-colored turf. Light-diamonds sparkled on the rippled surface of the water. I would never forget the pristine splendor this peaceful morning presented to me. Despite all the difficulty we might still encounter, I was glad to be alone on a rock with *nunatsiak* (the beautiful land) spread out before me.

Movement along the far shore caught my attention and I hurried to my packsack for my binoculars. I focused them on a bull caribou with a large rack still in velvet prancing along the shore. He was a fine specimen and I knew he would be very fat as he prepared for the impending rut.

I watched for a while then reluctantly gathered my tools and climbed into the greasy engine compartment to work on the motor. I cleaned and dried the exterior and drained the fuel tank. Finally I removed the engine cover and inspection plates to see if water had leaked into the crankcase or pistons. I was pleasantly surprised. Everything looked good with no evidence of water whatsoever. I replaced everything and drained the oil from the crankcase. There wasn't enough spare oil to bring it back up to the full mark. We would have to travel at reduced speed until we could get some more.

I was tired and hungry when I returned to the cabin and set about making a meal. I felt a sense of relief knowing that the motor was sound and with care should get us back over the 150 kilometers to the settlement.

As I sat in the cabin looking out at the river I noticed the canoe returning. I took my teacup and walked down to the water.

'Where's all the meat?' I asked as the boys landed.

'Didn't see a thing,' Bob replied.

Over tea I told Bob and Boris about the bull caribou I had spotted on the opposite shore and the good news about the motor.

As the tide rose we reloaded the *Nowja* and towed it off a safe distance and dropped anchor. I refilled the fuel tank and bled the lines. It was time to try the engine. After several cranks it fired up and ran smoothly.

Back in the cabin we got into a discussion on why the boat sank.

'Maybe there was too much slack on the anchor line,' I suggested. 'The wind blew her around too close to shore and at low tide she tipped enough for the waves to come in.'

'I guess we'll never know for sure,' Boris surmised.

'I was sure we were far enough off when we anchored, but it was hard to tell in the dark,' I concluded.

'Well, let's go kill that caribou you were admiring,' Bob suggested.

A search along the shore where I had sighted the caribou proved fruitless. We went further inland and climbed a rocky ridge. The days were becoming noticeably shorter and already the sun was sinking fast toward the western horizon. We sat down on some rocks and scanned the land below. The river glistened in the rays of the departing sun.

'I'm going to practice my wolf call just for fun,' I said as I cupped my hands. I delivered a long mournful howl that echoed along the boulder-strewn ridge.

'Look at that!' Bob was pointing as he spoke down toward the river.

A kilometer or so further downstream from where I had first sighted him, the bull caribou stood up and began to walk slowly along the shore.

'He was laying down there all the time,' Boris said as we reached for our rifles.

'Let's try and cut him off, maybe we can get close enough for a shot.'

'You guys go ahead,' Bob said. 'I'll go get the canoe.'

Boris and I sprinted down off the ridge like two hunting hounds. The caribou would probably keep following the shore and we might be able to get ahead of him a bit and wait for a shot.

We hurried downhill and positioned ourselves behind some rocks. The caribou continued to cautiously follow the river. When he was almost opposite us, we opened fire. I was a long shot, but the bull went down; then got up again almost immediately and continued to trot along the shore.

'I'll go further down and try to cut him off again,' I yelled to Boris as we started running again. I was further upstream than Boris and the caribou must have picked up my scent. He turned and doubled back. Boris was waiting and finished him off.

It was getting dark fast as we worked feverishly to skin and gut the animal. We heard the kicker motor out in the river and we went to the edge of the water and lit matches to guide Bob in with the canoe. We loaded up and pushed off for the cabin. It was a mad scramble to get going as it was almost dark and the tide was going out. In our haste I left my binoculars sitting on a large rock. I didn't realize it until the next day when we were on our way home. I've wondered since if they might still be there, a mute reminder of our caribou hunt on the Quoich.

CHAPTER THIRTY-FIVE

Events Worth Remembering

I'm going home to the northland
That land clear and bright
Where the Northern Lights dance
On a clear winter night.

Home to the Northland

ONE ASPECT OF MY POSITION as Game Officer was to enforce the Northwest Territories Game Ordinance and Regulations. The approach I tried to follow in Baker Lake emphasized education and common sense. A heavy-handed initiative would only have resulted in alienation. I used every opportunity to explain how wasteful and careless use of wildlife would eventually work against the Inuit. There were very few violations that resulted in court action and those that did occur were not confined exclusively to Inuit hunters.

One particular case remains memorable. Maurice Thibauldeau had recently arrived from Quebec with his wife and family. He was by trade a garment factory manager and it was hoped he would get the local duffel parka shop up and running. He was an amiable fellow, always cheerful, and very hospitable. Iris and I enjoyed several evenings with the Thibauldeaus over the winter despite the fact his wife spoke only French.

In a small community, news of any importance circulates regularly. One afternoon I heard that Maurice, Roy Emery and David Owingaya had gone hunting. I wasn't concerned as I assumed David would be doing the hunting and Roy and Maurice were along for the trip. Neither held hunting licences. My attitude changed when I received information that Maurice had shot a Canada goose with a rifle.

'How could he be so stupid?' I lamented to Iris as she prepared supper. 'He must know the season is closed and you can't use a rifle anyway.'

'Well, he hasn't been here very long.' Iris reminded me.

'I know, but Roy or David must have known. Anyway, the whole town knows about it now so I'll have to charge him, as much as I dislike doing it.' I pulled on my parka. 'I don't know how long this will take so have your supper if I'm late.'

As I trudged toward Thibauldeau's house, my annoyance grew. 'Why would he put me in a spot like this?' I went in the porch and knocked. Maurice answered the door in his usual friendly manner and invited me in.

I stepped inside before I announced. 'I'm here as the Game Management Officer for the area. Word has got around that you shot a Canada goose with a rifle today. The season for waterfowl is closed and if you shot a goose you are in violation of the Migratory Birds Convention Act.'

After this mandatory speech I paused to catch my breath. Maurice's friendly demeanour was quickly replaced with one of incredulity.

I proceeded to recite the statutory declaration to Maurice as he stood with jaw agape.

'You may be charged with hunting during a closed season, you don't have to say anything in answer to the charge...' and so on to the end.

Maurice began his reply in French and then switched to English. 'But I didn't know...I didn't know...I didn't want to cause any trouble.'

By this time his wife stood in the kitchen door speaking to Maurice in French. The children, drawn by the commotion, gazed wide-eyed around their mother.

'Maurice, did you shoot a goose with a rifle today?'

'*Oui, oui*, I did shoot...but I didn't know...I didn't think I was causing trouble.'

'The story is all over town, I have no choice but to charge you. Where's the goose, I'll have to seize it as evidence?'

'Oh no!...No!' Maurice moaned, then translated something to his wife. She immediately began to cry and looked at me with pleading eyes. What she was saying in French I couldn't understand.

'Do you have to take the goose? Oh, please don't take the goose; come, I will show you!'

He waved me toward the kitchen and pushed past his wife. I went to the doorway and there sitting on the oven door was a large goose in a roaster pan, skilfully prepared and ready to cook.

'Please mlt me roast the goose; my wife, she worked so hard to prepare it!'

I knew that without the bird as evidence, 'my goose' would be cooked in court if the case was contested. His wife continued to sob and chatter away in French intermittently. I took a step toward the stove, then stopped. I needed time to think.

'Get the rifle and shells you used to kill the goose.'

Maurice quickly disappeared into the bedroom. He appeared immediately and handed me his rifle and a box of cartridges.

'Maurice, here's what I'm going to do. I'm charging you with hunting during a closed season. I'll phone you and let you know when to appear before the Justice of the Peace. I'm keeping your rifle and shells as evidence, but against my better judgment I'm going to let you and the family eat the goose.'

Relief was much in evidence on Maurice's face as he quickly translated to his wife.

'*Merci, merci!*' she repeated.

'Listen, Maurice, I'm issuing you a warning for hunting without a licence and using a rifle instead of a shotgun, so consider yourself lucky. Don't put me on the spot like this again.'

With his repeated apology and thankfulness ringing in my ears I left his house and headed to the office to secure the firearm. Of course, I had to relate the whole story when I got home.

'If they eat the goose, how are you going to prove he shot one?' Iris queried with a smirk, after she had heard the details.

'I probably won't be able to, but I just didn't have the heart to take that bird out of the roaster with Lisse standing there wailing like I was about to seize her first born or something…anyway, he'd better plead guilty if he knows what's good for him.'

Maurice did plead guilty and was assessed the minimum fine and court costs. His rifle was returned to him.

The Thibaudeau family stayed in Baker Lake a year before leaving for a similar posting in Portage-La-Prairie, Manitoba. I've often wondered what additional incidents Maurice might have initiated had he stayed longer. Maurice seemed to possess the propensity to generate trouble without meaning to. One of his capers almost resulted in three of us joining Wally Thom on the bottom of the lake.

It was well known that liquor brought in from Churchill, Manitoba, carried a Northwest Territories tax, which had to be paid before Transair would accept the shipment. The only exception to this was during sealift when residents quietly arranged for cases of beer to be put on the ship and brought in without the tax being assessed. A beer shipment was too costly to bring in on the plane due to the weight.

The RCMP were aware this violation occurred every fall but kindly looked the other way. It was one of the few perks that residents of the community were able to take advantage of.

Maurice had generously agreed to consolidate the orders for everyone in town and began canvassing people on the phone list. Acting completely within character, he cheerfully phoned the RCMP members and inquired as to how many cases of beer they might be wanting tax-free? Maurice continually exhibited the most amazing naïveté to laws and regulations. The yearly tradition almost became history at this point until word filtered back that unless a greater degree of discretion was demonstrated the beer shipment would be seized.

One afternoon in late September the m.v. *Raven* was spotted steaming across the lake. Excitement spread through the community. Another sealift would soon be in full swing. It was reassuring to see the ship anchored offshore. It was like a silent link to the outside world. On board would be all the necessities and a few luxuries that would take us through the long winter ahead.

Several days after the ship arrived I got a phone call from Maurice as I was preparing to leave the office at the end of the day. Would I please run him out to the ship with my big canoe to pick up the beer order? I didn't think it would take long so I agreed and headed to the beach. In minutes Maurice arrived and helped me launch the eight meter flat-stern canoe.

The m.v. *Raven* rode at anchor about a half a kilometer off shore. The water was choppy and the temperature below freezing. Spray froze on my jacket as we made our way to the ship.

Maurice climbed the rope ladder to the deck while I remained with the canoe. After a brief wait, a sailor's face appeared over the rail and directed me to the bow of the ship where I was to receive the contraband. The cases started coming over the side as I watched the canoe settle deeper into the water.

'How many more?' I yelled up to the deck. 'I'm getting a good load here.' Obviously Maurice had miscalculated the thirst of the residents and the capacity of my canoe when he told me we could take it all in one trip.

'Just a few more!' Maurice yelled down, and followed the last of the cases into the canoe. By now the canoe was over the maximum cargo weight and I was concerned. As I reached for the starter rope Maurice yelled, 'There's a guy who wants to go to land!'

Before I could open my mouth to protest, a big husky sailor slid down a rope into the canoe. Now I was really worried. We were grossly overloaded and I was suckered into getting the canoe to shore.

I started the motor and gingerly eased away from the protection of the ship into the choppy offshore waves. One mistake and the canoe would swamp. The first wave broke at the bow, sending a mist of freezing spray over me. I gasped for breath, and prepared for the next one. Each wave had to be met perfectly. If we shipped any water over the side, the canoe would go down in seconds. Maurice and the sailor gripped the thwarts and stared at the on-coming waves. I gulped for air after each freezing shower and prayed that the motor would keep running.

Each breaking wave delivered a cloud of freezing spray. My jacket was encased in ice. The shore seemed too distant…the waves too high. For a brief moment I felt we wouldn't make it.

'We're going to swamp; I'm going to drown with a boat-load of booze.'

I'm certain it was only my many years of experience with canoes in rough lakes of Northern Saskatchewan that got us to shore safely. The canoe was so heavy it grounded in the shallows. I jumped into the frigid water and staggered to shore. The first stages of hypothermia were already being felt. My clothes were soaked and covered with ice. Maurice and the sailor in the bow of the canoe had managed to stay dry.

My voice was slurred from the cold as I yelled to Maurice, 'You guys get this on the beach, I'm going home!'

By the time I arrived my brain was fuzzy and I could barely walk. Later I would have plenty of time to consider the stupidity of risking my life for a canoe load of beer.

The opportunity to decline an all-expense-paid trip to the North Pole is something few people experience in a lifetime. Because I did exactly this on February 8, 1971, I feel it is worth explaining.

A peaceful Saturday afternoon dissolved in minutes when the Department of Transport radio communications' operator phoned and read me the following message:

MR LAND HAS BEEN CHOSEN TO ACCOMPANY A DANISH EXPEDITION TO THE NORTH POLE. REQUIRED TO PROCEED TO OTTAWA BY TUESDAY FEBRUARY 9. IF THERE IS NO SKED AUTHORIZED TO CHARTER OUT. IT HAS BEEN ARRANGED TO PAY FARE OUT TO WIFE'S PARENTS IF DESIRED. TRIP IS BY DOG TEAM. QUITE LARGE EXPEDITION. TAKE ALL ARCTIC GEAR.

P.A. KWATEROWSKY
SUPERINTENDENT OF GAME

Years later Paul Kwaterowsky would relate to me the conversation he had with the Director of the Department to which the Game Management Service belonged. Paul was called into his office late Friday afternoon to report on a suitable choice to send on the North Pole trek.

Alan Ballantyne asked Paul in his brusque ex-military manner, 'So who are we sending to the North Pole?'

Paul, who had a visible dislike of the Director, replied without hesitation, 'Why don't we send you, Mr Ballantyne?' The Director was not amused.

After receiving the message over the phone, I sank into a chair. Vaguely, I heard Iris asking in a concerned voice, 'What's wrong?'

'They want me to go to the North Pole.'

'What? Who wants you to go? What are you talking about?'

I repeated the contents of the message as I remembered it, and we discussed it for over an hour.

Finally Iris said, 'Well, you know *my* thoughts; you'll have to make the decision.'

'I'll have to get more information; if I say yes now, there'll be no way to get out later.' I prepared the following reply:

SUPERINTENDENT OF GAME.

RE: POLAR EXPEDITION. HONOURED TO BE ASKED. VERY DIFFICULT TO DECIDE ON PRESENT INFORMATION DUE TO IMPORTANCE OF MISSION. REQUIRE FURTHER FACTS BEFORE AN AFFIRMATIVE ANSWER CAN BE GIVEN.

1. ADVISE MY ROLE IN PARTY

2. ADVISE IF RETURN IS BY DOGS

3. ADVISE PLANS AND EXPERIENCE OF EXPEDITION MEMBERS

4. ADVISE IF SELF IS ONLY CANADIAN IN PARTY

5. ADVISE AIR SUPPORT AND COMMUNICATION

REGRET POOR SIGNALS. PLEASE ADVISE IF I SHOULD TAKE MONDAY SKED TO CHURCHILL FOR MORE DISCUSSION BEFORE FINAL DECISION

E. LAND
GAME MANAGEMENT OFFICER

I gave the message to Iris.

'I'm going to drop this off at the radio room and pick up the original radiogram.' Iris nodded and handed the message back.

It was late in the afternoon before I finally received the following reply:

ANSWER TO MOST OF YOUR POINTS NOT AVAILABLE BECAUSE OF LATE INSTRUCTIONS RECEIVED FROM OTTAWA. GAME OFFICER WILL BE THE ONLY CANADIAN PARTICIPANT. APPARENTLY HIGHLY QUALIFIED LARGE EXPEDITION, THREE TO FOUR HUNDRED DOGS TO BE USED FOR ENTIRE ROUND TRIP. NO DETAILS KNOWN RE: RADIO COMMUNICATIONS AS OF YET. YOU ARE TO REPORT IMMEDIATELY TO OTTAWA FOR BRIEFING THEN PROCEED ON THURSDAY BY CANADIAN AIRFORCE PLANE TO OTTAWA THE FOLLOWING THURSDAY FOR LAST MINUTE INSTRUCTIONS BY EXTERNAL AFFAIRS OR FOR OTHER NECESSARY ARRANGEMENTS. SUGGEST YOU CONTACT ME THROUGH MR MILLIGAN OR BAILEY WHO CAN RELAY MESSAGES AND BE PREPARED TO RENDER ALL NECESSARY ASSISTANCE TO YOU. WHEN YOU CALL ON MONDAY YOU WILL RECEIVE FURTHER INSTRUCTIONS TO WHOM TO REPORT IN OTTAWA

P. KWATEROWSKY

When Iris finished reading the message, I said. 'You know I really don't like the sound of this deal.'

'Are you going to go?'

'No, I'm not going!'

'I hope you won't regret it later.'

'Well, maybe I will, but this doesn't sit right with me, and I'm staying home.' I went to the table to prepare my reply.

As weeks passed, I learned more about the expedition I had turned down. It was being led by the Italian millionaire Guido Monzino. The party was made up of fourteen Inuit, three hundred dogs, two Italian mountain guides, a Chilean explorer and two Danes. Russ Hall from Game Management Headquarters took the position I was to have filled as a Canadian liaison representative on the trek.

The expedition was attempting to duplicate Robert Peary's first trip to the North Pole. The Inuit were from Kanak, north of Thule in Greenland, and some of them decided to leave the expedition taking ten sled teams with them. This occurred some 41 km out on the sea ice north of Cape Columbia. Russ Hall and one other member of the expedition were asked to withdraw when it became evident that the remaining dog sleds could not carry the eight original members. A Canadian Game Officer had been attached to the trek to carry a rescue beacon and to ensure the Greenland Inuit did not shoot polar bears. Monzino had posted a $50,000.00 bond with the Canadian Government to cover the cost of a rescue operation, should this become necessary.

Guido Monzino and his party did reach the North Pole on 19 May but failed to complete the return trip. On 11 June the expedition was flown off the floating ice-island called T-3 about 200 km south of the pole.

I never regretted my decision to stay at home and after talking with Russ on his return to Yellowknife, he assured me that all I missed was a lot of frustration.

CHAPTER THIRTY-SIX

Caribou Tagging

Where the caribou run and the bright midnight-sun
Casts its shadows in the valleys below
Where the wolf's lonely cry and the wind's weary sigh
Fill my heart with a joy one cannot know

Iyouweetuk

I ATTENDED A MEETING in Yellowknife which had been called to discuss the status of the various caribou herds. I listened as a Canadian Wildlife Service Biologist discussed the need for a caribou tagging project on the Thelon River. A previous tagging project had been carried out during the proclaimed caribou decline of the 1950s. The research scientist wanted to get some radio collars on caribou in the Beverly Herd in order to get some new data on numbers, movement and social interaction with other herds. He wanted to get started that summer (1972) but the logistics and costs seemed to preclude this.

I offered to haul the necessary supplies and equipment in to the cabin at Aberdeen Lake, thus greatly reducing their costs. The biologists seemed surprised and interested in this possibility. I assured them that I had already made trips into the area by Bombardier and sled and if they could cut the red tape and get some fuel and supplies purchased locally, I would haul it in for them.

Frank Miller assured me that I would be hearing from them without delay.

On 29 April I was once again on the now familiar trail to Aberdeen Lake. The first few trips were to set up fuel caches and then to haul the fuel necessary for the project to the site at Box Crossing on the Thelon River. The final trip was to haul the food supplies to the cabin.

Frank Bailey, despite the fact that he was now 62 years old, decided to accompany me.

Thomas Kakimut and Barnabus were also along.

We stopped at the cabin we had recently put up at Sissons Lake and

178

after we had a meal we pushed on across the lake. The drifts were rock hard and we had to cross more or less at a 90 degree angle so the going was pretty slow and very rough.

After several hours Frank dug around in his pack-sack and hauled out some cans of Coke. He pulled out his hunting knife and proceeded to stab some holes in the cans. I saw him wielding his hunting knife at the Coke which he held on the edge of his seat and I yelled above the roar of the engine, 'Do you want me to stop?'

'No, I'm all right, keep going.' Frank replied as he stabbed at the can to make a second hole. I slowed down as much as I could without stopping. Frank passed the can back to Kakimut and began operations on a second can. The bouncing Bombardier and Frank's big knife was making me nervous. He finished punching the second can and passed it back to Barnabus. As he was rummaging for a third can I heard Barnabus and Kakimut laughing, speaking in Inuk-tit-tuut and holding the can up inspecting the bottom. I glanced back and started laughing. On the bottom of the can was a pull-tab. Frank had the cans upsidedown. We all had a good laugh with Frank joining in before we pulled the tabs on the two remaining cans of Coke.

Frank insisted on doing his share of the driving and I could quickly see that he had handled Bombardiers for many years. He knew how to get the best out of the machine despite the heavy load on the sled.

As we crossed an open area of tundra before we reached Aberdeen Lake I saw an object in the distance. The light was hitting it in such a way that it looked like a building out in the middle of nowhere. It was close to our route so I headed over for a closer look. As we drew near we could see that it was a huge boulder sitting alone on this otherwise flat stretch of tundra. It was about five meters tall and seven to ten meters wide. Near the top was a little shelf in the rock face where a raptor bird had built a nest.

We stood and gazed at this lone monument for several minutes. It was very unusual as no other rocks could be seen nearby. I had Frank pose for a photograph beneath the raptor's nest before we finally got back into the Bombardier and pushed on.

This proved to be a very enjoyable trip. The weather was bright and sunny and the wind light. The vastness of the beautiful barren-lands opened before us like a good book inviting us to take the time to read. As always, schedules and the pressure of an impending transfer to Inuvik dictated that I should not linger longer than necessary. It was with some bitterness I unloaded the supplies at the cabin at Aberdeen Lake, realizing that I would not be a part of this project. In my mind I could see the caribou swimming strongly in the Thelon at Box Crossing and the rush of the

Frank Bailey beside large rock on open tundra. Raptor nest above him.

men to the canoes to intercept. I longed again to see the tundra in summer and see the heat waves rolling across a land alive with birds and animals. I knew that this great wild land had become fixed in my mind forever. Though I knew I must leave, I was sure I would never forget.

This was to be my last trip on the land with my friends, and I couldn't help feeling a little melancholy.

The spring of 1972 arrived with great anticipation. Things had never been better for us as a family or for me concerning the work and the country I had grown to love. We now lived in a new house and I had an office and a shop in a new building. The old decrepit Bombardier had been replaced with a new model and in place of an old leaky canoe, I had a new one with a 20 hp kicker to push it. Things that I had worked hard to achieve during the last four years were finally bearing fruit. So it was like a 'bolt from the blue' that word came in early April of an impending transfer to Inuvik.

After my initial anger had subsided, I prepared a long letter to my supervisor explaining as rationally as possible why this was not a good idea. At this point I wanted neither a promotion nor a transfer. Things were fine just as they were. None of my arguments prevailed and the transfer date loomed closer. I began to feel that perhaps Iris wanted a change and I was being somewhat selfish. After all it was she who was left at home with the children while I was out romping around on the tundra like a young caribou. We both began to prepare for the inevitable.

It would be a difficult departure without a doubt. We would be leaving behind close friends and countless memories. Special memories and special people like Betty Humphrey and Elizabeth Kotelewetz who had delivered our daughter Tavia in the local Nursing Station. It would be an emotional time to be sure.

I still had several trips to make to the Sandhills land camp north of Schultz Lake to complete the last cabin for a family who planned to move out there to live full time. The last of the sections were cached at the half-way point and I wanted to finish the job before I had to leave. I managed to get my transfer date set back to the middle of May.

There was an igloo winter camp at the Sandhills and on my last trip I went to the camp to say good-bye. When we arrived the people came out of the igloos to greet us. The camp had been set up in early fall and after a long winter of blowing snow, the camp was invisible from above except for some fox and wolverine pelts strung on a rope between tall poles in the snow.

I was digging out some grub from the back of the Bombardier and when I finally got out, Barnabus and the others had disappeared into the igloo. The wind was gusting up a ground drift as I searched around for the igloo entrance. I eventually found it and dove down the tunnel into instant blackness. Being somewhat larger than my Inuit friends I found the tunnel a tight squeeze. As I squirmed down the very long tunnel I noticed, as my eyes grew accustomed to the darkness, that it took a slight turn to the left. I began to wiggle around the corner when I felt my elbow strike something hard. I glanced down and there, inches from my elbow, was a large double-spring #4 trap set to spring. I remembered the habit of the last one out of the igloo moving the traps to the middle of the tunnel in case a wolverine decided to pay a visit. I found another at the doorway to the igloo. That trap would have done a real number on my elbow. I had been lucky.

When I entered everyone was visiting and laughing, sitting around on the sleeping platform which was comfortably covered with a thick layer of Arctic heather, willows and topped with caribou skins. The sun beamed through the ice block window dispelling the darkness. It was a very large igloo, over three meters high at the top of the dome. Another small igloo adjoined this one and I could see it was well stocked with caribou meat and fish. Soon the tea was ready and we continued to visit as we feasted. I knew that this would be my last visit so I especially valued the friendship and hospitality that was being expressed. I took a careful look around as we prepared to leave for I realized that I might never experience this culture again.

As if to dispel any lingering doubts we might have had about leaving Baker Lake on transfer, the wind shrieked across the ice strip on our departure date driving granular snow like lead shot against our faces. Iris had our daughter in her *amoutik* and I held Kevin tightly in my arms as we fought our way up the steps of Transair's Hawker-Sidley 748 Turbo-prop. We were leaving our home and friends of four years. New horizons beckoned. We would come back again for a short period, but nothing would ever be the same again. This was our home; and we were leaving something of ourselves behind.